SECOND GRADE TECHNOLOGY

32 LESSONS EVERY SECOND GRADER CAN ACCOMPLISH ON A COMPUTER

FIFTH EDITION

Part Three of Nine of the SL Technology Curriculum

Fifth Edition 2013
Part Three of Structured Learning's nine-volume Technology Curriculum
Visit the companion site http://askatechteacher.com© for more tech resources

Your wiki number is SECOND5-84-11. Use this to access free resources here

To receive free technology tips and websites, send an email to admin@structuredlearning.net with the message "Subscribe to Weekly Tips and Websites"

ISBN 978-0-9787800-2-9

Printed in the United States of America by Structured Learning LLC

Introduction

The educational paradigm has changed. New guidelines (most recently, the National Board of Governors Common Core Standards) expect technology to *facilitate learning through collaboration, publishing, and transfer of knowledge*. Educators want students to use technology to *work together, share the products of their effort, and employ the skills learned in other parts of their lives*.

How do we as teachers facilitate collaboration-publishing-transfer of knowledge?

We do it with the Structured Learning Technology Curriculum as roadmap. Aligned with Common Core State Standards* and National Educational Technology Standards, and using a time-proven method honed in classrooms, students learn the technology that promotes literacy, critical thinking, problem-solving, and decision-making. The purpose is not to teach step-by-step computer skills (like adding borders, formatting a document, creating a blog). There are many fine books for that. What this curriculum does is guide you to providing the **right information at the right time**. Just as most children can't learn to read at two, or write at four, they shouldn't be required to place hands on home row in kindergarten or use the internet before they understand the risks and responsibilities. We make sure students get what they need at the right age. The end result is a phenomenal amount of learning in a short period of time.

Fifth Edition 2013
Part One of Structured Learning's Technology Curriculum

Visit the companion site http://askatechteacher.com© for more tech resources

Your wiki number is K5-30-48. Use this to access *free resources here*

To receive free technology tips and websites, send an email to admin@structuredlearning.net with the message "Subscribe to Weekly Tips and Websites"

If there are skills you as teacher don't know, visit our Help blog (AskATechTeacher.wordpress.com) and co-teaching wikis:

- K-3rd grade — http://smaatechk-3.wikispaces.com/
- 4th grade — http://smaatech-fourthgrade.wikispaces.com/
- 5th grade — http://smaatech.wikispaces.com/

…for free help (use wiki number on book face page for access—see inset). Both are staffed by tech teachers ready to help you.

What's in the SL Technology Curriculum?

Here's what you'll find:

- *Experiential learning with real-world applications*
- *Inquiry-based projects, exercises and assignments*
- *Collaboration among students and teachers*

- *Opportunities for students to express and grow in their creativity*
- *International mindedness*

Here's a quick overview of what is included in this textbook:

- *Scope and Sequence of skills taught*
- *Step-by-step weekly lessons*
- *Monthly homework (3rd-5th only)*
- *Certificate of Completion for students*
- *Comprehensive list of websites to support learning*
- *Articles that address tech pedagogy*
- *Posters ready to print and hang on your walls*

Each lesson includes:

- *Common Core Standards**
- *ISTE Standards*
- *essential question*
- *big idea*
- *materials required*
- *vocabulary used*
- *problem solving for lesson*
- *time required to complete*
- *teacher preparation required*
- *steps to accomplish goals*
- *assessment strategies*
- *troubleshooting*
- *how to extend learning*
- *additional resources*
- *examples, grading rubrics*

Throughout the text are links to extend lessons, add enrichment, and/or provide flexibility in your teaching. No PDF? Google the website or contact our help sites.

Programs Used in these Textbooks

Programs used in this curriculum focus on skills that serve the fullness of a student's educational career. Free alternatives are noted where available:

General	K-2	3-8
Email	*Drawing program (or KidPix, TuxPaint)*	*Office (or Open Office, Google Docs)*
Google Earth	*Keyboard software or Free online site*	*MS Publisher*
Internet	*MS Office (or Open Office, Google Docs)*	*Adobe Photoshop (or Gimp)*
Web tools	*MS Publisher*	*Keyboard software or online tool*

What's New in the Fifth Edition?

A good curriculum is aligned with best practices. In technology, that means it must be updated every few years.

If you purchased SL's Fourth Edition, consider the following changes to technology in education since its 2011publication:

- *Windows has updated their platform—twice*
- *iPads are the device of choice in the classroom*
- *Class Smartboards are more norm than abnorm(al)*
- *Technology in the classroom has changed from 'nice to have' to 'must have'*
- *1:1 has become a realistic goal*
- *Student research is as often done online as in the library*
- *Students spend as much time in a digital neighborhood as their home town*
- *Textbooks are considered resources rather than bibles*
- *Teachers who don't use technology are an endangered species*
- *Words like 'blended learning', 'authentic', 'transfer', 'evidence' are now integral to teaching*
- *Common Core Standards have swept like a firestorm through the education community, most timed to take effect after 2011*

In response, here are changes you'll find:

- *Each lesson notes which **Common Core State Standard** is addressed*
- *Each lesson reflects Common Core emphasis on comprehension, problem-solving, critical thinking, **preparing students for career and college***
- *Students learn to **understand the process**, not just replicate a skill*
- *Lessons focus on **transfer of knowledge***
- ***Collaboration and sharing** is often required*
- *Online support is offered through **co-teaching wikis** and a **help blog***

Who Needs This Book

You are the Technology Specialist, Coordinator for Instructional Technology, IT Coordinator, Technology Facilitator, Curriculum Specialist, Technology Director, or tech teacher—tasked with finding the right project for a classroom. You have a limited budget, less software, and the drive to do it right no matter roadblocks.

Or you are the classroom teacher, a tech enthusiast with a goal this year—and this time you mean it—to integrate the wonders of technology into lessons. You've seen it work. Others in your PLN are doing it. And significantly, you want to comply with Common Core State Standards, ISTE, your state requirements, and/or IB guidelines that weave technology into the fabric of inquiry.

How do you reach your goal?

With this curriculum. It will give you confidence that your students are using technology for the blended learning required by state, national and international standards.

How to Use This Book

This technology curriculum is unlike others you've looked at. You are the guide for a class of learners. Lessons are student-centered and fluid, loosely presented as 4-6 week units, project- and skills-based. Depending upon age, units cover:

- *Word processing*
- *Desktop publishing*
- *Spreadsheets*
- *Presentations*
- *Internet use/Web-based tools*
- *Digital citizenship*
- *Google Earth*
- *Image editing*

A lesson is forty-five minutes. If there is a skill students don't get, spend additional time, especially when you see it come up a second or third time through the course of these textbooks. By the end of 8th grade, students have a well-rounded tech education that prepares them for college and/or career.

The table below tells you what's covered in which grade. Where units are taught multiple years, teaching reflects the Scope and Sequence, standards addressed, with increasingly less scaffolding and more student direction.

	Mouse Skills	Vocabulary - Hardware	Problem-solving	Windows and Basics	Keyboard and shortcuts	Word	Power Point	Publisher	Excel	Google Earth	Search/ Research	Graphics/ Visual Learning	Pro-gram'g	WWW	Robotics	Games	Dig Cit
K	☺	☺	☺	☺	☺					☺		☺		☺			☺
1	☺	☺	☺	☺	☺			☺	☺	☺		☺		☺			☺
2		☺	☺	☺	☺	☺	☺	☺	☺	☺		☺		☺			☺
3		☺	☺	☺	☺	☺	☺	☺	☺	☺	☺	☺		☺			☺
4		☺	☺		☺	☺	☺	☺	☺	☺	☺	☺		☺			☺
5		☺	☺		☺	☺		☺	☺	☺	☺	☺		☺			☺
6		☺	☺	☺	☺	☺	☺	☺	☺	☺	☺	☺		☺			☺
7		☺	☺	☺	☺	☺			☺	☺	☺	☺	☺	☺	☺	☺	☺
8		☺	☺	☺	☺	☺			☺	☺	☺	☺	☺	☺	☺	☺	☺

Here are a few hints:

- Teach lessons in the order presented in the book (for grades K-5). Lessons introduce, reinforce, and circle back on the concept. Certain skills provide scaffolding for others so you want them solid before moving on. Resist the urge to mix up lessons, even if it seems your perfect time for a particular project comes earlier/later than placement in the book.
- We understand what happens when kids and technology collide—sparks. Sometimes you can't move on because students are too excited about what they're doing. No problem. Two solutions:

- Leave the line in front of uncompleted activities blank and return to it another week when you have time. You'll notice after using this curriculum for a few years that your students will get through more material, faster.
- Take an extra week. Most school years run 35-40 weeks. This book includes 32 lessons. This works also if you miss a class due to a holiday or field trip.

- Always use lesson vocabulary. Students gain authentic understanding of word use by your example.
- 'Teacher Preparation' often includes chatting with the class teacher. Why?

  - You want to tie your class conversations in with her/his inquiry.
  - You want to offer sponge websites for early-finishers that address her/his topics.

- Expect students to be risk takers. Don't rush to solve their problems. Ask them to think how it was done in the past. Focus on problems listed in the lesson, but embrace all that come your way.
- Throughout the year, circle back on lessons learned. It takes students five times seeing a skill to get it—

  - First: They barely hear you
  - Second: They try it
  - Third: They remember it
  - Fourth: They use it outside of class
  - Fifth: They tell a friend

  Remind students throughout the year that they've learned the skills, are using them, and understand them. Check off skills in the Scope and Sequence additional times as you circle back on them.
- Join hundreds of teachers using the curriculum on our teaching wikis (links above). See how they handle issues. Ask questions. It's run by an educator who has used the curriculum for years. She'll help you. The only requirement is that you own this book.
- Need more help? Go to Ask a Tech Teacher©, our help blog (http://askatechteacher.com) run by a teacher using the curriculum.

Typical 45-minute Lesson

As you face a room full of eager faces, remember they learn best by doing.

"Tell me and I'll forget.
Show me and I may remember.
Involve me and I'll understand."
—Chinese Proverb (or Ben Franklin)

Don't take over the student's mouse and click for them or type in a web address when they need to learn that skill. Even if it takes longer, guide them to the answer so they know the path. If you've been doing this since kindergarten, you know it works. In fact, by the end of kindergarten, you saw remarkable results.

Here's how I run a class in the lab:

- Students start with 10 minutes of typing practice either on installed software or an online keyboarding program. Some days, youngers work instead on alphabet sites such as Bembo's Zoo or Starfall Letters (Google for websites).
- If it's the end of a grading period, I review which skills have been accomplished (see Scope and Sequence).
- If we are starting a new project, I review it, take questions and we start. If we are in the middle of one, students use the balance of class to work towards completion. I monitor activities, answer questions, help where needed. This portion of class is student-centered requiring critical thinking and problem-solving skills.
- As often as possible, I give younger students two weeks to finish a project—one to practice, one to save/export/print. This redundancy reinforces new skills and mitigates stress. If they are on week two, preparing to save/export/print, we start the day with the project and finish with typing to be sure students have as much time as possible to work.
- Students who complete the current project take advantage of age-appropriate 'sponge activities' from a topic that ties into class inquiry. I list websites on a class internet start page© (see inset for example of mine). Students know websites on this page can be used during sponge time.

Here are useful pieces to making your class tech productive and clear:

- *Textbook—the roadmap. Enough said.*
- *Class internet start page—enables you to provide a weekly update of what will happen in class complete with links and extensions. My students use this every time we're in class. It also provides a place to collect groups of links so you can direct students there quickly without recreating the list.*
- *Class wiki—provides detail on what happened during each class. You can also provide additional student and parent resources to enrich learning. Great for transparency with stakeholders and students who missed class.*

Copyrights

About the Authors

Structured Learning IT Team *is the premier provider of technology instruction books and ebooks to education professionals including curriculums, how-to guides, theme-based books, and a one-of-a-kind online helpline—all tools required to fulfill tech demands of the 21st century classroom. Materials are classroom-tested, teacher-approved with easy-to-understand directions supported by online materials, websites, blogs, and wikis. Whether you are a new teacher wanting to do it right or a veteran educator looking for updated materials,* **Structured Learning** *and its team of technology teachers is here to assist.*

Ask a Tech Teacher *is a group of technology professionals who run an award-winning resource* **blog**. *Here they provide free materials, advice, lesson plans, pedagogical conversation, website reviews, and more to all who drop by. The free newsletters and website articles help thousands of teachers, homeschoolers, and those serious about finding the best way to maneuver the minefields of technology in education.*

*Throughout this text, we refer to Common Core State Standards. We refer to a license granted for *"...a limited, non-exclusive, royalty-free license to copy, publish, distribute, and display the Common Core State Standards for purposes that support the Common Core State Standards Initiative. These uses may involve the Common Core State Standards as a whole or selected excerpts or portions.*

Table of Contents

Introduction

Technology Scope and Sequence K-6

Lesson Plans

Appendices

Articles

Posters

K-6 TECHNOLOGY SCOPE AND SEQUENCE©

Aligned with ISTE Standards

Check each skill off with I/W/M/C under ''ISTE' as students accomplish it
('ISTE' refers to the ISTE Standard addressed by the skill)

ISTE		I-Introduced; W-Working on; M-Mastered; C-Completed							
I		**Creativity and Innovation**	**K**	**1**	**2**	**3**	**4**	**5**	**6**
		Students demonstrate creative thinking, construct knowledge, develop innovative processes using tech							
		Apply existing knowledge to generate new ideas, products, or processes	I	W	W	W	M	C	C
		Create original works as a means of personal or group expression	I	W	W	W	M	C	C
		Use models and simulations to explore complex systems and issues	I	W	W	W	M	C	C
		Identify trends and forecast possibilities	I	W	W	W	M	C	C
		Graphics							
		Use software (i.e., KidPix) and web-based drawing platforms	I	W	M	C	C	C	C
		Know how to insert images from internet			I	W	M	C	C
		Know how to insert images from clipart			I	W	M	C	C
		Know how to import images from a file			I	W	M	C	C
		Know how to wrap text around an image			I	W	M	C	C
		Know how to resize/move/crop an image			I	W	M	C	C
		Know how to add borders			I	W	M	C	C
		Excel							
		Know how to add data to a cell				I	W	M	C	C
		Know how to add color to a cell				I	W	M	C	C
		Know how to add graphics to a worksheet				I	W	M	C	C
		Explore a business using models/simulations to study complex systems						I	W	M
		KidPix							
		Draw geometric shapes and format	I	W	M				
		Put student drawings into a slideshow	I	W	M				

	1	2	3	4	5	6
Use fonts to communicate ideas	I	W	M			
Know how to mix text and graphics to convey student's unique message	I	W	M			
Learn about tools, toolbars, mouse skills	I	W	M			

Scratch

	1	2	3	4	5	6
Apply existing knowledge to generate new ideas, products, or processes					I	W
Create/add/edit sprites					I	W
Add sound					I	W
Add text bubbles					I	W
Add backgrounds					I	W
Add movement					I	W
Complete program task cards for most common skills					I	W
Broadcast sprites					I	W
Use models created by others; remix to develop unique Scratch video					I	W

Robotics

	1	2	3	4	5	6
Contribute to project teams to produce original works or solve problems					I	
Build a robot					I	
Program a robot					I	
Trouble shoot simple problems					I	
Use sensors to monitor environment					I	
Measure distances with robots					I	

Web 2.0 Tools

	1	2	3	4	5	6
Know how to use models and simulations to explore complex systems				I	W	M
Be comfortable using web-based tools to convey knowledge		I	W	M	C	C	C

2 Communication and Collaboration

Students use digital media and environments to communicate/ work collaboratively, including at a distance, to support individual learning and contribute to the learning of others.

	1	2	3	4	5	6
Interact, collaborate, and publish with peers, experts, or others employing a variety of digital environments and media			I	W	M	C	C
Communicate information and ideas effectively to multiple audiences using a variety of media and formats	I	W	M	C	C	C
Develop cultural understanding and global awareness by engaging with learners of other cultures	I	W	M	C	C	C

	Col1	Col2	Col3	Col4	Col5	Col6	Col7
Contribute to project teams to produce original works or solve problems			I	W	M	C	C
Learn to scaffold classwork with technology tools		I	W	M	C	C	C

Vocabulary

	Col1	Col2	Col3	Col4	Col5	Col6	Col7
Understand content-specific vocabulary	I	W	M	C	C	C	C
Understand vocabulary relevant to computers in general	I	W	M	C	C	C	C
Communicate information, ideas effectively to multiple audiences using a variety of media, formats	I	W	M	C	C	C	C

Mouse Skills

	Col1	Col2	Col3	Col4	Col5	Col6	Col7
Know how to click, double-click, hold, drag, hover	I	W	M				
Use right mouse button		I	W	M	C	C	

Keyboarding

	Col1	Col2	Col3	Col4	Col5	Col6	Col7
Know how to use lab software	I	W	M	C	C	C	C
Know how use internet sites	I	W	M	C	C	C	C
Keyboard to grade-appropriate speed and accuracy				I	W	M	C
Use touch typing				I	W	M	C
Compose at keyboard				I	W	M	C
Understand handwriting speed vs. keyboard speed				I	W	M	C
Use curved hand, reach, correct hand			I	W	W	M	C
Use correct posture, elbows at sides	I	W	M	C	C	C	C
Know parts of keyboard—keys, numbers, F keys, arrows, Escape			I	W	M	C	C
Find period key, Shift, spacebar, tab	I	W	M				

Digital Storytelling

	Col1	Col2	Col3	Col4	Col5	Col6	Col7
Tell a story using different tools			I	W	M	M	C
Contribute to project teams to produce original works or solve problems			I	W	M	C	C

Word Processing

	Col1	Col2	Col3	Col4	Col5	Col6	Col7
Know how to Interact, collaborate, and publish with peers				I	W	M	C
Know when to use a word processing program			I	W	M	C	C
Use classroom writing conventions when word processing on computer	I	W	M	C	C	C	C
Know MS Word basics			I	W	M	C	C

Know page layout basics			I	W	M	C	C
Know how to add a watermark, pictures, graphic organizer					I	W	M
Know correct spacing after sentences, paragraphs		I	W	M	C	C	C
Know how to use grade-appropriate heading on Word docs			I	W	M	C	C
Know how to use the thesaurus					I	W	M
Know how to insert header, footer, bullet list, border, table			I	W	M	C	C
Know to put cursor in specific location, i.e., for graphic			I	W	M	C	C
Know how to select and then do—two-step process in editing, formatting			I	W	M	C	C
Know how to compose at Keyboard			I	W	M	C	C
Know how to use embedded link (Ctrl+Click)				I	W	M	C
Use Ctrl+Enter to force a new page			I	W	M	C	C

Publisher

Can identify parts of Publisher screen			I	W	M	C	C
Know when to use a desktop publishing program to share information			I	W	M	C	C
Know how to make a card, flier, cover page, magazine			I	W	M	C	C
Know how to insert an image, page, text box, border, header, footer, TofC			I	W	M	C	C
Know when to use a desktop publishing program to share information			I	W	M	C	C
Know how to plan a publication				I	W	M	C
Know how to work with font schemes, color schemes			I	W	M	C	C

Presentations

Know how to create a Windows slideshow	I	M					
Know when to use PowerPoint			I	W	M	C	C
Know how to add/rearrange slides			I	W	M	C	C
Know how to insert background, pictures, text boxes			I	W	M	C	C
Know how to add animations, movies (GIF's), transitions			I	W	M	C	C
Know how to auto-advance			I	W	M	C	C
Understand how to deliver a professional presentation			I	W	M	C	C

Blogs

Interact, collaborate, publish with peers employing a variety of digital media				I	W	M	C

Develop global awareness by engaging with learners of other cultures						I	W	M	C
Contribute to project teams to produce original works or solve problems								I	W

Robotics

Contribute to project teams to produce original works or solve problems								I	W

Web 2.0 Tools

Communicate information, ideas effectively to multiple audiences using a variety of media, formats					I	W	M	C	C
Use web-based communication tools to share student's unique and individual ideas on a subject					I	W	M	C	C
Learn a variety of tools by teaching them to classmates					I	W	M	C	C

Collaboration

3 Research and Information Fluency

Students apply digital tools to gather, evaluate, and use information

Evaluate/select information sources/digital tools based on appropriateness to specific tasks	I	W	M	C	C	C	C		
Learn how to collect information (Snippit, screen shots, etc.)					I	W	M	C	C

Internet

Know elements of a web address—www, http, .com					I	W	M	C	C
Know how to use internet effectively	I	W	M	C	C	C	C		
Understand website layout	I	W	M	C	C	C	C		
Plan strategies to guide inquiry by knowing how to choose links and menus	I	W	M	C	C	C	C		
Locate, analyze, evaluate internet sources					I	W	M	C	C
Know how to read search results					I	W	M	C	C
Locate, organize, analyze, evaluate, synthesize, and ethically use information from a variety of sources and media	I	I	I	W	M	C	C		
Copy-paste data/images from internet to doc					I	W	M	C	C
Evaluate and select information sources and digital tools based on appropriateness to specific tasks					I	W	M	C	C
Process data and report results using a variety of internet websites					I	W	M	C	C
Know how to use online tools to guide inquiry					I	W	M	C	C
Use a variety of internet websites to support classroom units	I	W	M	C	C	C	C		
Search for text on a page with Ctrl+F						I	W	M	C

	Interact comfortably with internet activities		I	W	M	C	C	C	C

Google Earth								
	Display familiarity with tools	I	W	M	C	C	C	C
	Know how to find a location, save picture, import into another tool	I	W	M	C	C	C	C
	Know how to process data/share results from tours and searches					I	W	C
	Understand latitudes and longitudes				I	W	M	C
	Know how to use ruler to measure distances					I	W	C
	Know how to individualize a placemark					I	W	C
	Know how to run/create a tour			I	W	M	C	C

Publisher								
	Know when to use Publisher			I	W	M	C	C
	Know how to add/edit text, add/delete page, add/delete picture, insert footer			I	W	M	C	C
	Know how to work with font schemes, color schemes			I	W	M	C	C
	Know how to plan a publication, make a flier, trifold, newsletter, cover page				I	W	M	C

Excel								
	Understand basics		I	W	W	M	M	C
	Process data, report results by collecting data into Excel				I	W	M	C
	Know how to add text, graphics, data				I	W	M	C	C
	Know how to use paint bucket fill				I	W	M	C	C
	Know how to use formulas					I	W	M	C
	Know how to label x and y axis on graphs					I	W	M	C
	Know how to name a chart					I	W	M	C
	Know how to recolor tabs; rename worksheets					I	W	M	C
	Know how to sort data alphabetically					I	W	M	C
	Know how to use Excel to analyze a business						I	W	M
	Know how to publish Excel to blog, website						I	W	M

Web 2.0								
	Use Web 2.0 tools to enhance learning			I	I	W	M	C

Research								

	Plan strategies to guide inquiry			I	W	M	C	C
	Can locate, organize, analyze, evaluate, synthesize, and ethically use information from a variety of sources and media	I	W	M	C	C	C	C
	Can evaluate and select information sources and digital tools based on the appropriateness to specific tasks		I	W	M	C	C	
	Can process data and report results		I	W	M	C	C	
	Know how to limit search to find what is needed			I	W	M	C	
	Know how to take notes from internet for a project			I	W	M	C	

4 Critical thinking, Problem solving and Decision making

Students use critical thinking skills to plan and conduct research, manage projects, solve problems, and make informed decisions using appropriate digital tools and resources

	Plan and manage activities to develop a solution or complete a project that coordinates with classroom units	I	W	M	C	C	C	C
	Use multiple processes, diverse perspectives to explore solutions	I	W	M	C	C	C	C

Critical thinking

	Understand how to identify/define authentic problems/questions to investigate	I	W	M	C	C	C	C
	Understand terminology for computer hardware	I	W	M	C	C	C	C
	Understand the purpose of Start button, clock, desktop	I	W	M	C	C	C	C
	Understand that class computer pod is just like computer lab	I	W	M	C	C	C	C
	Attempt to solve a problem before asking for teacher assistance	I	W	M	C	C	C	C
	Know how to print to a different location		I	W	M	C	C	C
	Know why you save to network folder	I	W	M	C	C	C	C
	Know how to use programs not taught		I	W	C	C	C	C
	Know the difference between save and save-as		I	I	I	W	M	C
	Know the difference between backspace and delete		I	I	I	W	M	C
	Understand differences between tool bars	I	W	M	C	C	C	C

Problem solving

	Identify and define authentic problems, questions for investigation	I	W	M	C	C	C	C
	Know user name and password	I	W	M	C	C	C	C
	Know how to determine date	I	W	M	C	C	C	C
	Use keyboard shortcuts as alternatives			I	W	M	C	

		Know what to do if double-click doesn't work	I	W	M	C	C	C	C
		Know what to do if document disappeared	I	W	M	C	C	C	C
		Can visually compare own screen with instructors	I	W	M	C	C	C	C
		Know how to undo	I	W	M	C	C	C	C
		Follow established procedure when asking for help	I	W	M	C	C	C	C
		Know what to do if part of computer doesn't work	I	W	M	C	C	C	C
		Use Alt+F4 to shut down frozen program				I	W	M	C
		Use Task Manager to shut down locked program				I	W	M	C
		Know how to solve specific common problems	I	W	M	C	C	C	C
		Know how to access work from anywhere in school	I	W	M	C	C	C	C
		Know how to print, save	I	W	M	C	C	C	C
		Know how to Open a document, close a document	I	W	M	C	C	C	C
		Can solve common computer problems without assistance				I	W	M	C
		Use Alt+F4 to shut down frozen program				I	W	M	C
	Decision Making								
		Know how to follow directions	I	W	M	C	C	C	C
		Identify and define authentic problems and questions for investigation					I	W	M
		Collect, analyze data to identify solutions and make informed decisions	I	W	M	C	C	C	C
		Know which program is right for which tasks	I	W	M	C	C	C	C
	Blogging								
		Able to create blogs for journaling and tracking project progress				I	W	M	C
		Able to incorporate text, images, widgets to better communicate ideas				I	W	M	C
	Websites								
		Use websites to publish work and share with others						I	W
		Use media from various sources to communicate ideas			I	W	M	C	C
		Share unique understanding of ideas and concepts						I	W
5	**Digital citizenship**								
Students understand human, cultural, societal issues related to technology/practice legal and ethical behavior									
		Understand the concept of 'digital citizenship'	I	W	M	C	C	C	C

Computers and Society							
Advocate and practice safe, legal, and responsible use of information	I	W	M	C	C	C	C
Know what an 'online presence' is	I	W	M	C	C	C	C
Understand plagiarism and how to avoid it					I	W	M
Exhibit a positive attitude toward technology that supports collaboration learning, and productivity	I	W	M	C	C	C	C
Demonstrate personal responsibility for lifelong learning	I	W	M	C	C	C	C
Understand the importance of citing sources			I	W	M	C	C
Understand the concept of 'cyber-bullying' and how to avoid it	I	I	I	I	W	M	C
Exhibit leadership for digital citizenship—set the standard for classmates	I	W	M	C	C	C	C
Understand 'Cloud computing'				I	W	M	C
Recognize irresponsible and unsafe practices on internet				I	W	M	C
Internet							
Know correct use of internet	I	W	M	C	C	C	C
Know how to use links, back button, home button , scroll bars	I	W	M	C	C	C	C
Know how to copy-paste data	I	W	M	C	C	C	C
Know how to how to evaluate a website					I	W	M
Search/Research							
Know how to search effectively and efficiently				I	W	M	C
Know how to limit search to find what you need				I	W	M	C
Know how to identify reliable resources				I	W	M	C
Know how to search for text on a page				I	W	M	C
Web 2.0							
Understand Cloud computing						I	W
Use models and simulations to explore complex systems and issues						I	W	M
Use Web 2.0 tools to enrich understanding and learning			I	W	M	C	C
Computer etiquette							
Understand netiquette rules	I	W	M	C	C	C	C
6 **Technology operations and concepts**							

Students demonstrate a sound understanding of technology concepts, systems, and operations							
Understand and use technology systems	I	W	M	C	C	C	C
Select and use applications effectively and productively	I	W	M	C	C	C	C
Transfer current knowledge to learning of new technologies	I	W	M	C	C	C	C
Use network folders, school technology	I	W	M	C	C	C	C
Use blogs for student journaling, digital portfolios				I	I	I	W
Use Google Apps, Google Sites				I	I	I	W
Hardware							
Know hardware names and parts of keyboard	I	W	M	C	C	C	C
Can connect parts to tower	I	W	M	C	C	C	C
Can understand difference between power buttons on monitor and tower	I	W	M	C	C	C	C
Can use computer volume button	I	W	M	C	C	C	C
Windows							
Understand concept of Desktop, taskbar, start button, icons, task manager	I	W	M	C	C	C	C
Know how to use Windows to run a slideshow	I	W					
Know how to log on, open/close programs, save	I	W	M	C	C	C	C
Understand how to add file folders					I	W	M
Know how to use tool tips				I	W	M	C
Understand right-click menus				I	W	M	C
Know how to copy-paste from one program to another				I	W	M	C
Know how to drag-drop between folders					I	W	M
Know how to access different drives from Explorer	I	I	I	I	I	W	M
iPads							
Use class set of iPads	I	W	M	C	C	C	C

Lesson #1—Introduction

Vocabulary	Problem solving	Big Idea
▪ *CPU* ▪ *Digital* ▪ *Internet start page* ▪ *Mouse wheel* ▪ *Peripheral* ▪ *Port* ▪ *Power buttons* ▪ *Right-click*	▪ *Double-click doesn't work (push enter)* ▪ *Monitor doesn't work (check power)* ▪ *Volume doesn't work (check plugs)* ▪ *Headphones don't work (are they plugged in?)*	*Students develop an awareness of computer components, fundamental hardware issues, and basic computer operations*
Time Required *45 minutes*	**NETS-S Standards** *4a, 6a*	**CCSS** *CCSS.ELA-Literacy.SL.2.1a*

Essential Question
How do I use the computer?

Overview

Materials

Internet, websites on class start page, last year's class rules

Teacher Preparation

- Tie into classroom conversations where possible
- Have a list of class rules that worked in past years. Have a marker to add student suggestions to list
- Test equipment so students aren't frustrated trying something that won't work
- Is class shorter than 45 minutes? Highlight items most important to your integration with core classroom studies and leave the rest for 'later'
- Ensure that required links are on lab computers

Steps

_____Tour classroom so students become comfortable in the place they'll visit every week.

_____Discuss why students use technology.

_____Collect class rules from students (see sample set at end of lesson) including:

- *Save early, save often—every 10 minutes*
- *No food or drink around computer*
- *Respect the work of others and yourself*

_____Include class discussion guidelines such as:

- *listen to others*
- *take turns while speaking*
- *wait to be called on before speaking*

_____Review hardware:

- *Mouse buttons—left and right, double click, scroll; how to hold mouse*
- *CPU—power button, disk drives, connections*
- *Monitor—power button, screen*
- *Headphones—volume, port*
- *Keyboard—see next pages for important keys*
- *Peripherals—what are those?*

_____As you teach, incorporate lesson vocabulary. Check this line if you did that today!

_____Throughout class, check for understanding. Expect students to solve problems and make decisions that follow class rules.

_____Remind students to transfer knowledge to classroom or home.

_____Tuck chairs under desk, headphones over tower; leave station as you found it.

Assessment Strategies
- *Anecdotal observation*

Trouble-shooting:
- *If there are hardware problems, have students try to solve them before you assist.*
- *You have print book and need website? Pick grade level and search (Alt+F) name on https://askatechteacher.wordpress.com/great-websites-for-kids/.*

Extension:
- *Students who finish can visit class internet start page (see a discussion on Start Pages at end of lesson) for technology practice websites; If you have pdf, try these:*

  - *Computer basics*
  - *Computer Basics II*
  - *Computer Insides*

  - *Computer puzzle*
  - *Find the Technology*

- *If this lesson doesn't work for your students, use one from **How to Jumpstart the Inquiry-based Classroom.** It has 5 projects aligned with SL curriculum.*

More Information:
- *We often suggest discussing issues with students. This is part of an inquiry-based classroom. For more on that, check the article at the end of this lesson.*
- *Lesson questions? Go to http://askatechteacher.com*
- *Second grade teaching wiki:*
  http://smaatechk-3.wikispaces.com/This+Week+in+Tech—Second+Grade
- *PDF: See appendix for bonus websites*
- *Follow keyboard lessons in K-8 Keyboard Curriculum (http://ow.ly/j6GH8)*

If you don't get through everything, check completed items so you know what to get back to when you have time on later lessons. I find as I focus on the central idea of a lesson, clarifying questions sometimes take more time than I'd expect. I'm fine with that. There'll be lessons later that move faster than I planned.

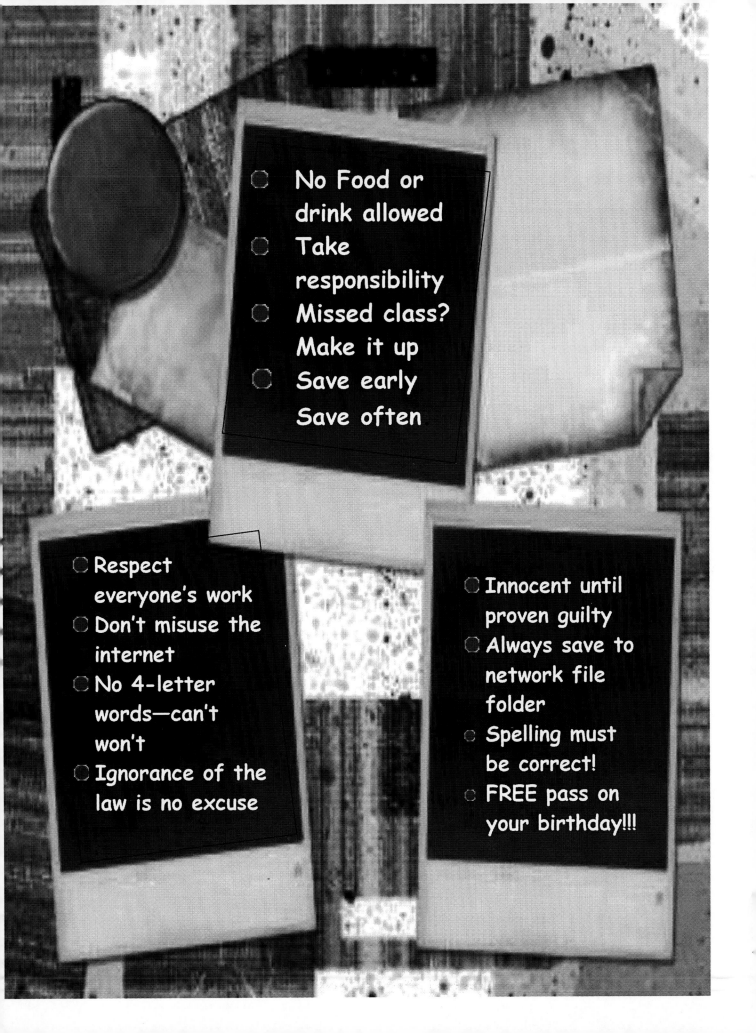

Using an Internet Start Page

An internet start page is the first page that comes up when students select the internet icon. It should include everything students visit on a daily basis (typing websites, research locations, sponge sites) as well as information specific to the current project, class guidelines, the day's 'to do' list, and a calculator. It is one of the great ways teachers can make internetting simpler and safer for their students.

Mine includes oft-used websites, blog sites, a To Do list, search tools, email, a calendar of events, pictures of interest, rss feeds of interest, weather, news, a graffiti wall and more. Yours will be different. I used protopage.com, but you can use netvibes or Symbaloo.

Start pages are an outreach of the ever-more-popular social networking. They typically have a huge library of custom fields to individualize any home page. And, they're all simple. Don't be intimidated.

When you get yours set up, on the To Do list, put what the child should do to start each computer time. This gives them a sense of independence, adultness, as they get started while you're wrapping something else up.

10 Ways to be an Inquiry-based Teacher

It's hard to run an inquiry-based classroom. Don't go into this teaching style thinking all you do is ask questions and observe answers. You have to listen with all of your senses, pause and respond to what you heard (not what you wanted to hear), keep your eye on the Big Ideas as you facilitate learning, value everyone's contribution, be aware of the energy of the class and step in when needed, step aside when required. You aren't a Teacher, rather a guide. You and the class move from question to knowledge together.

Because everyone learns differently.

Where your teacher credential classes taught you to use a textbook, now it's one of many resources. Sure, it nicely organizes knowledge week-by-week, but in an inquiry-based classroom, you may know where you're going, but not quite how you'll get there—and that's a good thing. You are no longer your mother's teacher who stood in front of rows of students and pointed to the blackboard. You operate well outside your teaching comfort zone as you try out a flipped classroom and the gamification of education and are thrilled with the results.

And then there's the issue of assessment. What students accomplish can no longer neatly be summed up by a multiple choice test. When you review what you thought would assess learning (back when you designed the unit), none measure the organic conversations the class had about deep subjects, the risk-taking they engaged in to arrive at answers, the authentic knowledge transfer that popped up independently of your class time. You realize you must open your mind to learning that occurred that you never taught—never saw coming in the weeks you stood amongst your students guiding their education.

Let me digress. I visited the Soviet Union (back when it was one nation) and dropped in on a classroom where students were inculcated with how things must be done. It was a polite, respectful, ordered experience, but without cerebral energy, replete of enthusiasm for the joy of learning, and lacking the wow factor of students independently figuring out how to do something. Seeing the end of that powerful nation, I arrived at different conclusions than the politicians and the economists. I saw a nation starved to death for creativity. Without that ethereal trait, learning didn't transfer. Without transfer, life required increasingly more scaffolding and prompting until it collapsed in on itself like a hollowed out orange.

So how do you create the inquiry-based classroom? Here's advice from a few of my efriend teachers:

1. *ask open-ended questions and be open-minded about conclusions*
2. *provide hands-on experiences*
3. *use groups to foster learning*
4. *encourage self-paced learning. Be open to the student who learns less but deeper as much as the student who learns a wider breadth*
5. *differentiate instruction. Everyone learns in their own way*
6. *look for evidence of learning in unusual places. It may be from the child with his/her hand up, but it may also be from the learner who teaches mom how to use email*
7. *understand 'assessment' comes in many shapes. It may be a summative quiz, a formative simulation, a rubric, or a game that requires knowledge to succeed. It may be anecdotal or peer-to-peer. Whatever approach shows students are transferring knowledge from your classroom to life is a legitimate assessment*
8. *be flexible. Class won't always (probably never) go as your mind's eye saw it. That's OK. Learn with students. Observe their progress and adapt to their path.*
9. *give up the idea that teaching requires control. Refer to #8—Be flexible*
10. *facilitate student learning in a way that works for them. Trust that they will come up with the questions required to reach the Big Ideas*

In the end, know that inquiry-based teaching is not about learning for the moment. You're creating life-long learners, the individuals who will solve the world's problems in ten years. You're job is to ensure they are ready.

Lesson #2—Introducing Tools and Toolbars

Vocabulary	Problem solving	Big Idea
▪ Alt ▪ Backspace ▪ CPU ▪ Ctrl ▪ Desktop ▪ Double-click ▪ Enter ▪ Icon ▪ Keyboard ▪ Log-on ▪ Palette ▪ Peripherals ▪ Port ▪ Shortkeys ▪ Spacebar ▪ Toolbars ▪ Tools ▪ Tower ▪ USB	▪ My mouse doesn't work (wake it) ▪ My mouse doesn't work (is red light underneath it lit?) ▪ My volume doesn't work (are headphones plugged in?) ▪ Double-click doesn't work (push enter) ▪ Computer doesn't work (check power) ▪ My monitor doesn't work (is it on? Is mouse awake?) ▪ I can't close the program (Alt+F4) ▪ How often do I save (save early save often) ▪ I can't find the tool (try shortkey) ▪ My drag-and-drop doesn't work (use left mouse button, not right) ▪ I can never find the tool (try shortkeys)	*Apply existing knowledge to generate new ideas, products, or processes*
Time Required 45 minutes	**NETS-S Standards** 3a, 6a	**CCSS** Anchor standards

Essential Question
How do tools and toolbars help me use the computer?

Overview

Materials

Internet, graphics program (i.e., KidPix, TuxPaint), keyboard program, shortkey list, common keys diagram

Teacher Preparation

- Talk with classroom teacher so you tie into class conversations
- If keyboard program requires student accounts, have that done by today
- Is class shorter than 45 minutes? Highlight items most important to your integration with core classroom studies and leave the rest for 'later'.

Steps

_____Discuss major parts of computer—CPU, monitor, keyboard, mouse, headphones, volume, printer, power buttons, USB ports, peripherals. Show how they connect to computer. Discuss trouble-shooting hardware problems:

- *if volume doesn't work, check headphones and volume control*
- *if mouse doesn't work, is it lit up (which means mouse works)*

- *If keyboard doesn't work, does NumLock work (which means keyboard works)*
- *if headphones don't work, are they plugged in? In correct CPU?*
- *If monitor doesn't work, is it on? Is mouse awake?*
- *If computer doesn't work, is it on? Is it hibernating?*

_____Discuss important keys (see poster at end of lesson—and discuss shortcut keys like Alt and Ctrl) students should know by the end of this year. Model them with students.

_____Discuss shortkeys students are familiar with (see next pages for most common):

- *Ctrl+P*
- *Ctrl+S*
- *Alt+F4*

- *Ctrl+V*
- *Ctrl+C*
- *Alt+Tab*

_____Practice keyboarding using software or online website (see appendix for suggestions).

_____Before beginning, discuss proper posture—hands on home row, legs in front of body, elbows at sides, keyboard in front of body, mouse to right (or left if appropriate). Remind students to use:

- *thumb for spacebar*
- *finger closest to key for letters*

_____Done? Open drawing program (KidPix, free TuxPaint, other). Art programs are great to teach mouse skills, tools, and toolbars. They're fun so students practice skills.

_____What are tools? Toolbars? Which ones do students remember from prior years?

_____Allow students to explore program.

_____As you teach, incorporate lesson vocabulary. Check this line if you did that today!

_____Throughout class, check for understanding. Expect students to solve problems as they maneuver through lesson and make decisions that follow class rules.

Assessment Strategies
- *Anecdotal observation*
- *Used prior knowledge*
- *Followed directions*
- *Joined class conversations*

_____Close to desktop (Alt+F4); leave station as it was (chairs in, desktop clean, monitor on, headphones over tower).

_____Remind students to transfer knowledge to classroom or home.

_____Tuck chairs under desk, headphones over tower; leave station as you found it.

Trouble-shooting:
- *Students turn monitors off so they don't have to figure out how to close programs? Have students leave monitors on at end of class.*
- *If students have trouble remembering where tools are, remind them of shortkeys that accomplish the same goal.*
- *If there are hardware problems, have students try to solve them before assisting.*
- *Sometimes you need more than one week for a lesson. No worries. There are 32 lessons in text, 35ish in school year. Feel free to stretch a lesson a week or more.*

- *You have print book and need website link? Pick grade level and search (Ctrl+F) name on https://askatechteacher.wordpress.com/great-websites-for-kids/.*

Extension:

- *Replace this lesson with 2nd Grade lesson #2 How to Animoto in curriculum extendors (http://www.structuredlearning.net/book/k-6-curriculum-extender/).*
- *Replace with 2nd Grade Lesson #3 Why is Digital Privacy Important? in curriculum extendors (http://www.structuredlearning.net/book/k-6-curriculum-extender/).*
- *Students who finish can visit class start page for websites that go with class inquiry.*

More Information:

- *There's a secret to teaching tech to a room-full of beginners: It's called 'delegate'. Read more about it in the article at the end of this lesson.*
- *Lesson questions? Go to http://askatechteacher.com*
- *Second grade teaching wiki: http://smaatechk-3.wikispaces.com/This+Week+in+Tech—Second+Grade*
- *PDF: See appendix for bonus websites*
- *Follow keyboard lessons in K-8 Keyboard Curriculum (http://ow.ly/j6GH8)*

If you don't get through everything, check completed items so you know what to get back to when you have time on later lessons. I find as I focus on the central idea of a lesson, clarifying questions sometimes take more time than I'd expect. I'm fine with that. There'll be lessons later that move faster than I planned.

IMPORTANT KEYBOARD KEYS

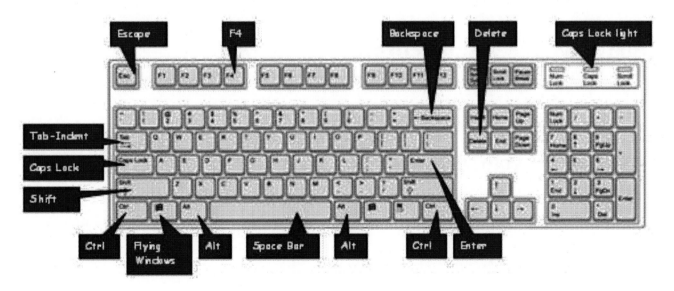

KEYBOARD SHORTCUTS

Maximize window   Double click title bar

Quick Exit   Alt+F4

Date and Time   Shift+Alt+D = Date

     Shift+Alt+T = Time

Show taskbar   WK (Windows key)

Show desktop   WK+M

Ctrl Key Combinations

CTRL+C: Copy   CTRL+K: Add hyperlink

CTRL+X: Cut   CTRL+E: Center align

CTRL+V: Paste   CTRL+L: Left align

CTRL+Z: Undo   CTRL+R: Right align

CTRL+B: Bold   CTRL+P: Print

CTRL+U: Underline   CTRL+ : Zoom in Internet

CTRL+I: Italic   CTRL- : Zoom out Internet

CTRL+P: Print

Fun Keyboard Shortcuts:

‹ +=+ › = ⇔

— + › = →

:+) = ☺

Add Your Favorite:

_____

_____

Should Tech Teachers be in the Classroom or the Lab

The following question was posed by one of my blog readers:

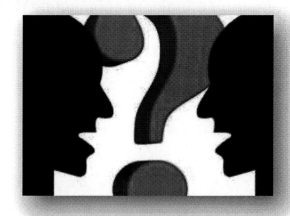

I teach lower school computer class to grades 1-4 at a private school in Columbus, Ohio. Our Technology Vision for 2015 is to get the students out of the computer lab, where they now learn computer skills based on classroom themes, and move me into the classroom where I would be the "technology integration teacher" alongside the classroom teacher. I would help with SmartBoard, IPad, laptop lessons integration, etc. I think this is a good idea and have been told that this is the trend in education but have not gotten real clarity on why and how this transition should take place.

Here are my questions: Do you see the benefit of technology integration into classrooms as I stated above? Is this the trend in education? If so why and how do you make this big transition? My feeling is that students need to learn computer skills such as formatting a document, searching the web, tools within PowerPoint, etc...This is much easier in a lab setting than classroom. Should we have both a lab and an itinerant technology integration teacher?

I get this question often, not to mention how many times it pops up on my tech forums and Nings. Technology teachers as a group are struggling to identify and define their future role: Should they teach computer skills or are they to integrate technology into classroom inquiry (as required in Common Core)—or both. These are two disparate functions and as my reader suggests, accomplished differently.

- *To teach a technology curriculum that—as ISTE suggests—prepares students to be digital citizens, requires a gamut of skills not always conducive to classroom units. I can force almost any technology unit (say, Excel formulas) into a classroom topic, but it's not always best suited there. And, if the classroom teacher wants to use Excel formulas in a math unit, I need time to teach the **pre-skills** that prepare students to **use** the program (page layout, toolbars, a lovely unit I have on drawing in Excel that painlessly teaches its use).*
- *So much of moving tech into the classroom depends on the grade level teacher's skills. If s/he doesn't know how to use Glogster or create a trifold, how will those projects get finished?*
- *If you're lucky enough to have a class set of computers in each classroom, then the move is easier. If not—how do you efficiently teach five students at a time? Most of us don't have the*

time in our schedule to visit each class multiple times a week. And what if the classroom teacher considers your time in her classroom 'planning time' and leaves? Then what's the sense of moving into the classroom?

Teaching in the lab emphasizes the skills-based nature of a program. Moving technology into the classroom re-forms it as a project-based approach to support classroom inquiry with a multitude of demands on the classroom teacher to understand your field. One approach is a separate class (like Spanish and PE) with a curriculum. The other is a resource for classroom units. Philosophically, they are night and day.

And what about keyboarding? Students need to learn the proper way to type so they can efficiently and effectively complete the work of classroom tie-ins. Then there's the growing need to teach students to be good digital citizens. Where does this involved topic fit into classroom inquiry? And when?

My goal as a tech teacher has always been twofold:

1) *inspire a student's imagination—share the exciting tools that technology offers so learners can select what works for them.*
2) *offer instructional differentiation—if a student is more comfortable with art than writing, why shouldn't s/he communicate with a drawing?*

I want students to see how Publisher magazines are prepared, Google Earth book tours work, Scratch videos created. Then, when the need arises—when they're asked to communicate their thoughts—they can select which option works best for their particular learning style. This is student-directed, student-led learning. What could be more exciting?

The Secret to Teaching Tech: Delegate

There's a secret to teaching kids how to use the computer. It's called 'delegate'. I don't mean slough off teaching to aides or parents. I'm referring to empowering students to be problem-solvers, then expect it. Here's how:

- Computers are only hard to learn if kids are *told* they are. Don't. Compare keyboarding to piano—a skill lots of kids feel good about—or one that relates to your particular group. Remove fear.

- Teach students how to do the twenty most common problems faced on a computer (more on that as they get older). Expect them to know these—do pop quizzes if that's your teaching style). Post them on the walls. Do a Problem-solving Board. Remind them if they know these, they'll have 70% less problems (that's true, too) than kids who don't know how to solve these. If they raise their hand and ask for help, play Socrates and force them to think through the answer. Sometimes I point to the wall. Sometimes I ask the class for help. Pick a way that works for you. The only solution you *can't* employ is to do it for them

- Teach students keyboard shortcuts. Does that sound like an odd suggestion? It isn't. Students learn in different ways. Some are best with menus, ribbons and mouse clicks. Some like the ease and speed of the keyboard. Give them that choice. If they know both ways, they'll pick the one that works best for them. Once they know these, they'll be twice as likely to remember how to exit a program (Alt+F4) or print (Ctrl+P).

- Let neighbors help neighbors. I resisted this for several years, thinking they'd end up chatting about non-tech topics. They don't when sufficiently motivated and interested. They are excited to show off their knowledge by helping classmates.

Lesson #3—Meet Your Computer

Vocabulary	Problem solving	Big Idea
■ *Alt F4* ■ *Caps lock* ■ *Class start page* ■ *Ctrl+P* ■ *Desktop* ■ *Flying windows* ■ *Font* ■ *Icons* ■ *Network* ■ *Network folder* ■ *Right click* ■ *Shift key* ■ *Start button* ■ *Taskbar*	■ *My monitor doesn't work (check power)* ■ *Shift key doesn't work (Is caps lock on?)* ■ *I can't find the program icon (use 'search' on Start button)* ■ *How do I close a program (Alt+F4)* ■ *How do I print (Ctrl+P)* ■ *Taskbar's gone (push flying windows)* ■ *How do I get to class internet start page (help students understand this process)* ■ *I have to use Caps Lock to capitalize a letter (for one letter: Use Shift)* ■ *Why can't I touch my neighbor's mouse? (We want you to help—with your words)* ■ *Where's class internet start page (where was it last year?)*	***Students develop an awareness of computer components, fundamental hardware issues, and basic computer operations***
Time Required *45 minutes*	**NETS-S Standards** *1b, 2b*	**CCSS** *Anchor standards*

Essential Question
How do I use the computer?

Overview

Materials

Internet, drawing program, keyboarding software, printer

Teacher Preparation

- Tie into class discussions wherever possible
- Have websites on class internet start page to support class discussion on various topics
- Are program icons on desktop or start button? Or both?
- Is class shorter than 45 minutes? Highlight items most important to your integration with core classroom studies and leave the rest for 'later'

Steps

_____Discuss the proper care and feeding of a computer. Can students think of rules to add to the following list?

- *No food or drink around computer—not even water*
- *No banging on keyboard, monitor or any other part of computer*
- *Demonstrate how to help a neighbor: Use words, don't touch their computer parts—mouse, keyboard, etc.*

_____Review Windows:

- *Desktop—front of monitor, 'screen', icons*
- *Taskbar—bar at bottom of screen, with clock and 'Start' button*
- *Clock—on right side of taskbar (hover for date)*
- *Start button—click to bring up programs (or use flying windows key)*
- *Show students how to find network folders with Start button-Computer-Network (nested by grade, teacher—or however your school does it)*

_____Review hardware—monitor, CPU, keyboard, mouse, headphones, peripherals—and related problems.

_____Use drawing program (KidPix, TuxPaint, Kerpoof, or other) to explore how technology communicates ideas. Remind students: Grammar and spelling count in tech class:

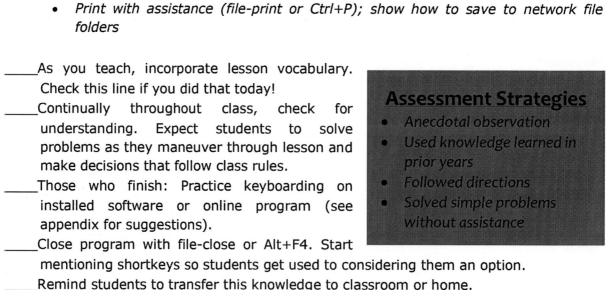

- *Open drawing program*
- *Enlarge font size to 72 and add 'My name is'; capitalize first letter; add student name with 'dog alphabet' (animation tool)*
- *Draw student picture with paint and pencil*
- *Print with assistance (file-print or Ctrl+P); show how to save to network file folders*

_____As you teach, incorporate lesson vocabulary. Check this line if you did that today!

_____Continually throughout class, check for understanding. Expect students to solve problems as they maneuver through lesson and make decisions that follow class rules.

_____Those who finish: Practice keyboarding on installed software or online program (see appendix for suggestions).

_____Close program with file-close or Alt+F4. Start

Assessment Strategies
- *Anecdotal observation*
- *Used knowledge learned in prior years*
- *Followed directions*
- *Solved simple problems without assistance*

mentioning shortkeys so students get used to considering them an option.

_____Remind students to transfer this knowledge to classroom or home.

_____Tuck chairs under desk, headphones over tower; leave station as you found it.

Trouble-shooting:
- *If there are hardware problems, have students try to solve them before assisting.*
- *You have print book and need website? Pick grade level and search (Alt+F) name on https://askatechteacher.wordpress.com/great-websites-for-kids/.*

- Student can't find drawing program? Use 'search' on Start button.
- Sometimes you need more than one week for a lesson. No worries. There are 32 lessons in the text, 35ish in the school year. Feel free to stretch a lesson a week or more.

Extension:
- Add stamps to picture of what students like most.
- Publish student work to class blog, wiki, website. Ask students to comment on the work of their classmates.
- Those who finish: Go to class internet start page and visit websites that tie into class conversations. If necessary, go over how to access this link with class
- In first few weeks of school, visit classrooms and help students understand that class computers are the same as tech lab—just smaller. See suggestions at end of lesson.
- Replace this lesson with 4th Grade Lesson #4 Book Review by Characters in curriculum extendors (http://www.structuredlearning.net/book/k-6-curriculum-extender/).

More Information:
- See article at end of lesson—"Do You Make These 9 Mistakes". This discusses the most common tech teacher mistakes. Do you make them?
- Lesson questions? Go to http://askatechteacher.com
- Second grade teaching wiki: http://smaatechk-3.wikispaces.com/This+Week+in+Tech—Second+Grade
- PDF: See appendix for bonus websites
- Follow keyboard lessons in K-8 Keyboard Curriculum (http://ow.ly/j6GH8)

If you don't get through everything, check completed items so you know what to get back to when you have time on later lessons. I find as I focus on the central idea of a lesson, clarifying questions sometimes take more time than I'd expect. I'm fine with that. There'll be lessons later that move faster than I planned.

Computing—the art of calculating how much time you wasted and money you spent in a doomed attempt to master a machine with a mind of its own.

Do You Make These 9 Mistakes

...with your students/child's computer education?

- Show how to do something rather than allowing her/him to discover
- Do for them rather than let them do it
- Say 'no' too often (or the other enthusiasm-killer, Don't touch!)
- Don't take them seriously
- Take technology too seriously. It's a tool, meant to make life easier. Nothing more.
- Underestimate their abilities
- Over-estimate their abilities
- Give up too quickly
- Think there's only one way to do stuff on the computer

I promise—none of these are necessary to thrive in technology. Children walk in the classroom loving learning. They can't break most computer parts. They *want* to try things out and do it themselves.

Let them. They may discover a Better Mousetrap.

After fifteen years, I still learn from my students. Children are serious about having fun. It's one of their jobs. Technology is how they do this. Feel free to join them. You'll be surprised how much they know.

But, sometimes, they need help. Offer it with a guiding hand.

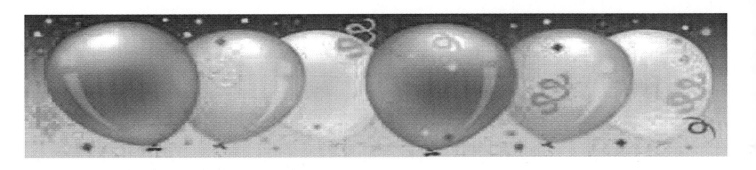

Take Tech into the Classroom

When the classroom teachers feels students are settled into the class routine enough to get started on the class pod of computers, make time to join them for center time and transfer tech class knowledge to the class.

Before going:

- Make sure the class computers work
  - *CPU*
  - *headphones*
- Make sure class computers have all links required for class work. What are the teacher's favorites?
  - *The school website*
  - *Tech lab class internet start page*
  - *Typing practice program*
  - *Starfall*
  - *A math program*
- Make sure they are set up the same as the tech lab (or know where the differences are so you can explain to students

During your visit, go over these with students:

- Same rules that apply in the tech class apply in the classroom (add your rules)
  - No *food or drink by computers*
  - *No fooling around*
  - *No grabbing neighbor's equipment*
  - *No internet except on approved sites*
  - *Try to solve problems before asking for help (especially important because you as tech teacher won't be there to help)*
  - *Read the screen before asking for help*
  - *Leave the station the way you found it*
  - *Print only with permission*
- Practice good habits every time you sit at computer
- Take questions

Lesson #4—Introduction to Google Earth

Vocabulary	Problem solving	Big Idea
3D Caps lock Double click Font Google Earth Icons Log on Street view Tool bar Zoom	*Volume doesn't work (check control)* *Monitor doesn't work (check power)* *What is date (check systray clock)* *How do I exit a program (Alt+F4)* *How do I use Street View (click SV guy and see which streets light up)* *Why can't I use Street View (it's not available everywhere)* *Buildings aren't 3D (is 3D layer selected? Are buildings 3D?)*	*Students use technology to identify and define authentic problems and significant questions for investigation*
Time Required *45 minutes*	**NETS-S Standards** *4a, 4d*	**CCSS** *CCSS.ELA-Literacy.RI.2.7*

Essential Question
How can I use technology to explore my world?

Overview

Materials

Internet, Google Earth on computers, drawing program, printer, keyboard website

Teacher Preparation

- Talk with classroom teacher prior to teaching this lesson so you can tie into a field trip coming up or a unit being studied
- Have keyboarding website on class internet start page
- Is class shorter than 45 minutes? Highlight items most important to your integration with core classroom studies and leave the rest for 'later'.

Steps

_____Practice keyboarding with a program that focuses on one row at a time. For the first three months of school, spend one month on each row: 1) home row, 2) QWERTY row, 3) lower row. My favorite sites: DanceMat Typing and Nimble Fingers (Google names for addresses). See checklist at end of lesson for anecdotal assessment.

_____Use correct hand position, legs in front, elbows at side. Review hints (see next pages) for better keyboarding, but dole them out as students are ready for them.

_____Open Google Earth. Discuss how this program uniquely contributes to and clarifies understanding of a topic:

- *Easily see a country's relationship to the world*
- *Zoom in or out to get a better perspective*
- *Drop into Street View to see firsthand what the world looks like*

_____Review program—zoom in/out, drag map, use street view, tour 3d buildings, use arrows. Give students time to remember skills from 1st grade and kindergarten.

_____Demo today's project:

- *Find sample country of origin*
- *Explore country. Use Street View and 3D layer for full experience*
- *Adjust view so country is recognizable on screen. Zoom in/out and drag map with mouse to display country nicely*
- *Take a picture with Google Earth and save to student folder*

_____Now it's student's turn to find their country of origin, adjust it and save image to network folder. Let them experiment with tools. Don't worry if it's not perfect.

_____When finished, give students time to explore their homeland.

_____Close Google Earth and open drawing program (we use KidPix). Expect students to remember how to use this program from last week and prior years.

_____Demonstrate this next stage of project:

- *Add saved image to canvas*
- *Add flag for student country of origin*
- *Add student name with ABC tool in any font, size 48, any color*

_____Now students do this.

_____As you teach, incorporate lesson vocabulary. Check this line if you did that today!

_____Throughout class, check for understanding. Expect students to solve and make decisions that follow class rules.

_____Save to network file folders with student last name and project name; print.

Assessment Strategies

- *Keyboarding observation (with/without checklist)*
- *Followed directions*
- *Used skills from prior years*
- *Understood how programs work together in project*
- *Solved simple problems without assistance*

_____Why is it important to put student name in file name? Demonstrate a search for students of their name. See how their files show up even if they didn't save it right—as long as they saved it to network? Putting a last name in file name makes it harder to lose work.

_____Remind students to transfer knowledge to classroom or home.

_____Tuck chairs under desk, headphones over tower; leave station as you found it.

Trouble-shooting:

- *If students have difficulty dragging globe, introduce arrow keys.*
- *If students have difficulty changing perspective, use tool on right side of screen.*
- *Computer doesn't work? Show student how hardware issues can cause problems. Don't fix it for them unless you must!*
- *You have print book and need website? Pick grade level and search (Alt+F) name on https://askatechteacher.wordpress.com/great-websites-for-kids/.*

- *Street View (or 3D) doesn't work? It's not available on all streets or buildings.*

Extension:
- *Use upcoming field trip instead of country of origin. Show route, measure distance, enter buildings if 3D available, travel streets if Street View available. Very fun.*
- *Use a geographic location that ties into classroom discussion instead of country of origin. As above, use 3D buildings and Street View to extend learning (if available).*
- *Explore other locations using Google's World of Wonder.*
- *Explore Universe or underwater by switching between Google Earth and Google Sky.*
- *Use time of day tool to show sunrise/sunset around globe.*
- *If class is discussing a historic event, use Time Slider tool to change date.*
- *Sometimes you need more than one week for a lesson. No worries. There are 32 in text, 35ish in school year. Feel free to stretch a lesson a week or more.*
- *If this lesson doesn't work for your student group, use one from **How to Jumpstart the Inquiry-based Classroom.** It has 5 projects aligned with the SL curriculum.*

More Information:
- *Lesson questions? Go to http://askatechteacher.com*
- *Second grade teaching wiki: http://smaatechk-3.wikispaces.com/This+Week+in+Tech—Second+Grade*
- *PDF: See appendix for bonus websites*
- *Follow keyboard lessons in K-8 Keyboard Curriculum (http://ow.ly/j6GH8)*

If you don't get through everything, check completed items so you know what to get back to when you have time on later lessons. I find as I focus on the central idea of a lesson, clarifying questions sometimes take more time than I'd expect. I'm fine with that. There'll be lessons later that move faster than I planned

Student _____

Keyboarding Technique Checklist*

Technique	Date	Date	Date	Date	Date
Feet placed for balance.					
Body centered to the middle of keyboard.					
Sit up straight.					
Follows directions.					
Completes exercises on time.					
Uses correct right or left hand for letters (1st Grade).					
Uses correct finger for each key reach (2nd Grade).					
WPM (words per minute) – 2nd Grade					
Accuracy percent – 2nd Grade					

4 pts	=	Mastery level	2 pts	=	Partial Mastery level
3 pts	=	Near Mastery level	1 pt	=	Minimal Mastery level

Credit: 'Bernadette Roche, Director of Technology for a Midwest independent school

Keyboarding Hints for K-2

1. Make sure the keyboard remains in front of the student and the mouse to the right (or left for lefties). Students want to push the keyboard out of the way so they can concentrate on the mouse. Don't let them. Make it a habit to keep the keyboard centered in front of their body with the mouse comfortably on the side

2. Have student tuck their elbows against the sides of their bodies. This keeps hands in the right spot—home row

3. Use thumb for the space bar. That leaves hands on home row

4. Curl fingers over home row—they're cat paws, not dog paws

5. Use inside fingers for inside keys, outside fingers for outside keys

6. Use the finger closest to the key you need. Sounds simple, but this isn't what usually happens with beginners.

7. Keep pointers anchored to f and j

8. Play keyboard like a piano (or violin, or guitar, or recorder). You'd never use the pointer for all keys

9. Fingers move, not hands. Hands stay anchored to the f and j keys

10. Don't use caps lock for capitals! Use shift.

11. Students must keep hands to themselves. Don't touch others mouse, keyboard, monitor. This gives them a sense of responsibility over their own station, knowing no one can touch it but them

12. Extra: Add a barrier between the sides of the keyboards. I fashioned one from cover stock. That reminds students to stay on the correct side of the keyboard

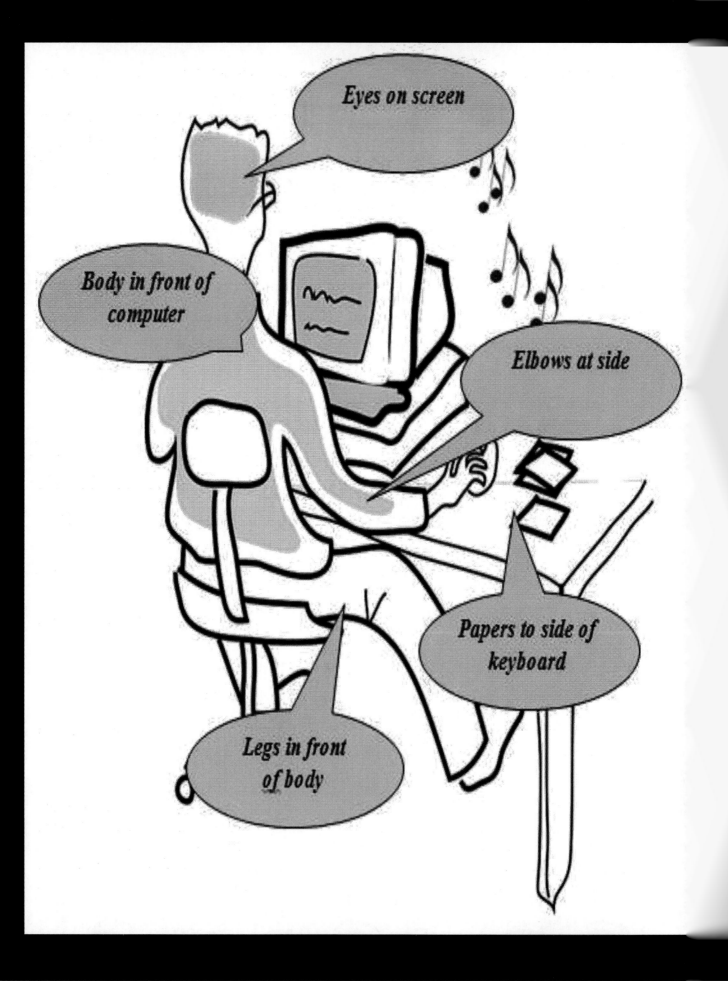

Lesson #5—Meet MS Word

Vocabulary	Problem solving	Big Idea
▓ Ctrl ▓ Cursor ▓ Edit ▓ Font ▓ Format ▓ Menu ▓ Number Square ▓ Password ▓ Return ▓ Reveal ▓ Ribbon ▓ Screen ▓ Show/hide ▓ Word ▓ Word processing ▓ Wrap	▓ How do I open a program (double click program icon) ▓ How do I close a program (Alt+F4 or file-exit) ▓ What's the difference between backspace and delete (see next pages) ▓ What's the difference between 'save' and 'save-as' (see next pages) ▓ What's the difference between 'edit' and 'format'? ▓ What's the difference between menu, ribbon, toolbar? ▓ Why must I have my name in file name?	*Students develop an awareness of basic computer operations*
Time Required *45 minutes*	**NETS-S Standards** *2b, 6a*	**CCSS** *CCSS.Math.Content.2.NBT.A.1a*

Essential Question
How do I communicate with a computer?

Overview

Materials

Internet, template for Number Square, MS Word or word processing program, Google Earth (if necessary), printer

Teacher Preparation
- Ask math teacher if students have learned the Number Square
- Have Number Square file available on network server
- Is class shorter than 45 minutes? Highlight items most important to your integration with core classroom studies and leave the rest for 'later'.

Steps

_____Students who haven't, finish Google Earth project. Those who completed it last week can practice home row on an online keyboarding website (see appendix). Remind students to use correct posture, hands on home row, keep elbows at sides.

_____This unit starts a 7-week unit to familiarize students with MS Word (or other word processing program like Google Docs, Open Office). It includes:

- *Intro to basics*

- *2 writing projects*
- *1 graphic organizer*

_____By the end of this unit, students will know Word basics that will get them through anything required in second grade.

_____Open Word on SmartScreen; review layout and demonstrate pieces:

- *appearance of screen*
- *tools and toolbars*
- *menus and ribbons students will use*
- *cursor: tells user where they are*

_____Discuss the difference between **menus, ribbons, toolbars,** and **taskbar**. Ask students for their thoughts. These organizational techniques are confusing. Be prepared to circle back on them often.

_____Open *Number Square* (see inset and sample at end of lesson) on SmartScreen. What is a number square? Is it familiar to students? Do they see how each row is a bundle of 10? How many is a bundle of ten tens? Discuss the place value of each digit in a number. Notice how each column is laid out (remember 'columns' from Excel).

_____Demonstrate how to type student name and teacher into blanks. If you're not in typeover, it will push line out. Demonstrate this and how to fix.

_____Review MS Word basics they will use today:

- *show where font size/color/type tools are*
- *discuss difference between backspace and delete (see next pages)*

_____Demo first line of Number Square:

- *fill in missing numbers*
- *change fonts as required in directions*
- *change colors as required in directions*
- *change font sizes as required in directions*

_____Don't expect students to finish project. The goal is to get comfortable using tools, changing fonts, formatting a document. These are skills they will use often.

_____As you teach, incorporate lesson vocabulary. Check this line if you did that today!

_____Throughout class, check for understanding. Expect students to solve problems as they maneuver through lesson and make decisions that follow class rules.

_____Save to network folder with student last name and project name. Print. Assist if required. What's the difference between 'save' and 'save-as' (see next pages)?

_____Why is it important to include student last name in file name (remember last week?)

_____Close program with file-close or Alt+F4; leave station as it was (chairs in, desktop clean, headphones over tower, text behind monitor).

_____Remind students to transfer this knowledge to the classroom or home.

Assessment Strategies

- *Anecdotal observation*
- *Followed directions*
- *Made connections between tens, digits, rows, columns*
- *Saved project in digital portfolio*

Trouble-shooting:

- *Hardware problems? Have students try to solve them before providing assistance.*
- *Occasionally when students have difficulty doing what you are teaching, ask why. And listen. You may be surprised by the answer.*
- *You have print book and need website? Pick grade level and search (Alt+F) name on https://askatechteacher.wordpress.com/great-websites-for-kids/.*
- *Sometimes you need more than one week for a lesson. No worries. There are 32 lessons in text, 35ish in school year. Feel free to stretch a lesson a week or more.*

Extension:

- *Show students how to align text in cells, add borders and pictures to cells.*
- *If this lesson doesn't work for your student group, use one from **How to Jumpstart the Inquiry-based Classroom.** It has 5 additional projects aligned with SL curriculum.*

More Information:

- *Lesson questions? Go to http://askatechteacher.com*
- *Second grade teaching wiki: http://smaatechk-3.wikispaces.com/This+Week+in+Tech—Second+Grade*
- *PDF: See appendix for bonus websites*
- *Follow keyboard lessons in K-8 Keyboard Curriculum (http://ow.ly/j6GH8)*

If you don't get through everything, check completed items so you know what to get back to when you have time on later lessons. I find as I focus on the central idea of a lesson, clarifying questions sometimes take more time than I'd expect. I'm fine with that. There'll be lessons later that move faster than I planned.

Number Square

Name: _____ Teacher_____

1. Fill in missing numbers
2. Color every multiple of 2 red
3. Change font on numbers that end in 7 to Comic Sans
4. Color every multiple of '3' blue
5. Change font size for all multiples of 9 to 24

1	2	3			7			10
	12			15	16				20
		23		25		27		29	
	32		34	35		37			40
41	42	43			46		48	49	
51	52				56	57			60
			65					69	70
71		73			76				
	82	83					88		
91			94						100

Difference between 'Save' and 'Save-as'

WHAT'S THE DIFFERENCE BETWEEN SAVE AND SAVE AS?

SAVE

- Save the first time
- Resave changes to the same location

SAVE AS

- Resave under a new name
- Resave to a new location

Difference between 'Backspace' and 'Delete'

TWO WAYS
TO DELETE

Deletes to the left, one character at a time

Deletes to the right, one character at a time

Lesson #6—Halloween Greeting I

Vocabulary	Problem solving	Big Idea
▓ *Cursor* ▓ *Digital portfolio* ▓ *Drill down* ▓ *Edit* ▓ *F keys* ▓ *Font color* ▓ *Font size* ▓ *Format* ▓ *Grammar* ▓ *Green lines* ▓ *Heading* ▓ *Network* ▓ *PDF* ▓ *Red squiggly lines* ▓ *Title*	▓ *What if log-on doesn't work?* ▓ *What if password doesn't work?* ▓ *I can't find my doc (try 'My Documents')* ▓ *How do I open a program* ▓ *How do I close a program* ▓ *What's the difference between backspace and delete* ▓ *When do I save or save-as* ▓ *What's the difference between 'edit' and 'format'?* ▓ *What's the difference between a heading and a title?* ▓ *How do I move down a line (push enter)*	*I can use computers to share thoughts*
Time Required *45 minutes*	**NETS-S Standards** *2b, 6b*	**CCSS** *CCSS.ELA-Literacy.W.2.3*

Essential Question
How do I use the computer to communicate?

Overview

Materials

Internet, MS Word or word processing program

Teacher Preparation
- Understand writing rules taught in core class so you can support those
- Talk with classroom teacher: Is there a topic students could write a letter about?
- Have websites on class internet start page that tie into class conversations
- Is your class shorter than 45 minutes? Highlight items most important to your integration with core classroom studies and leave the rest for 'later'.

Steps

_____Discuss writing. What strategies have they learned for success in writing? With student input, develop a list of skills students will use during this exercise.

_____What is the difference between writing by hand and on a computer? Consider 1) trying to remember where keys are, 2) typing while thinking, 3) hand gets tired, 4) handwriting is slow 5) computer typing is slow in 2nd grade, 6) which is harder/easier? Discuss how all of these might change as they get older.

_____Discuss difference between typing from a written copy and typing from thoughts in student's head. Which is harder? The students' answers may surprise you.

_____Today, students start a two-week project writing a story in MS Word (or Google Docs or Open Office—whatever word processing program your school uses). Show sample inset. Students always get excited by colors, fonts, clipart. They don't believe they'll be able to do this in two weeks!

_____Open MS Word. Review last week skills: fonts, sizes, insert, tools, toolbars

_____Remind students they will use same writing skills here they use for class literacy projects.

_____Add heading at top (name, teacher, date). Why a heading? Add two enters to leave room for the title. That will be added later.

_____Change font to 48. Sentence starts with capital, ends with period; space after period/ comma. What other writing rules did class come up with that should be used today?

_____Follow class strategies for story writing (i.e., Bold Beginning, Mighty Middle, Exciting Ending). Start with an introduction (i.e., Once upon a time, there was a ghost...), tell a bit about the story characters, tell what problem they faced and how they solved it. Include details to describe actions, thoughts, and feelings. Use temporal words to signal event order. Provide a sense of closure. Three-four sentences are fine.

_____Every time students sit at computer, remind them to use good keyboarding skills—correct posture, elbows at sides, mouse to right (or left), keyboard centered.

_____Show students how to verify story fits one page and adjust font size if needed.

_____Correct red (spell-check) and green (grammar) squiggly lines When do they use backspace or delete to make corrections? What are the blue squiggly lines—can students figure that out?

_____Add title. How do students know the title? Discuss how it comes from story. Discuss writing 'headlines' and 'titles'—that they draw reader in and make them want to continue.

_____When done, work with a neighbor. Read through each other's story and suggest edits.

_____Continually throughout class, check for understanding. Expect students to solve problems as they make decisions that follow class rules.

_____Have students take their time during this project. Here, they learn many Word basics.

_____As you teach, incorporate lesson vocabulary. Check this line if you did that today!

_____Save to network file folder with student last name and project name. Do they 'save' or

Assessment Strategies

- *Saved project to digital portfolio*
- *Joined class conversations*
- *Wrote an interesting title*
- *Transferred knowledge of skills from prior lessons*
- *Followed Common Core and class writing conventions*

'save-as'? What's the difference? Why must their last name be in the file name?

_____Close to desktop. Remind students to transfer knowledge to classroom or home.

_____Tuck chairs under desk, headphones over tower; leave station as it was.

Trouble-shooting:

- *If there are hardware problems, students try to solve before asking for help.*
- *You have print book and need website? Pick grade level and search (Alt+F) name on* https://askatechteacher.wordpress.com/great-websites-for-kids/.
- *Sometimes you need more than one week for a lesson. No worries. There are 32 lessons in text, 35ish in school year. Feel free to stretch a lesson a week or more.*

Extension:

- *Offer inquiry-based websites on class internet start page for students who finish early.*
- *Replace with Third Grade Lesson #2 Puzzle Maker to Prepare for Tests in* curriculum extendors *(http://www.structuredlearning.net/book/k-6-curriculum-extender/).*

More Information:

- *Lesson questions? Go to* http://askatechteacher.com
- *Second grade teaching wiki:* http://smaatechk-3.wikispaces.com/This+Week+in+Tech—Second+Grade
- *PDF: See appendix for bonus websites*
- *Follow keyboard lessons in* K-8 Keyboard Curriculum *(http://ow.ly/j6GH8)*

If you don't get through everything, check completed items so you know what to get back to when you have time on later lessons. I find as I focus on the central idea of a lesson, clarifying questions sometimes take more time than I'd expect. I'm fine with that. There'll be lessons later that move faster than I planned.

> **"Pencil and paper**: archaic information storage and transmission device that works by depositing smears of graphite on bleached wood pulp. Requires operator skilled at *'handwriting'* technique."

Is Keyboarding Dead?

I was on one of my tech teacher forums—where I keep up to date on changes in education and technology—and stumbled into a heated discussion about what grade level is best to begin the focus on typing (is fifth grade too old—or too young?). Several teachers shared that keyboarding was the cornerstone of their elementary-age technology program. Others confessed their Admin wanted it eliminated as unnecessary. Still others dismissed the discussion as moot: Tools like Dragon Speak (the standard in speech recognition software) and iPhone's wildly-popular Siri mean keyboarding will soon be as useful as cursive and floppy discs.

My knee jerk reaction was *That's years off,* but it got me thinking. Is it really? Or are the fires of change about to sweep through our schools? Already, families are succumbing to the overwhelming popularity of touch screens in the guise of iPads. No typing required—just a finger poke, a sweep, and the command is executed. Those clumsy, losable styluses of your parent's era are so last generation. The day kids discover how easy it is to *tell* their phones what they need done (think iPhone 4S)—stick a fork in it; keyboarding will be done.

Truthfully, as someone who carefully watches ed tech trends, a discussion about the importance of keyboarding says as much about national education expectations as typing. Schools are moving away from reports and essays as methods of assessing understanding. Teachers want plays that act out a topic, student-created videos that demonstrate authentic understanding, multi-media magazines that convey a deeper message. Web-based communication tools like Voki, Animoto, and Glogster—all of which have limited typing—are *de rigeu*r in every academic program that purports to be tech-savvy. Students are encouraged to use audio, visual, taped vignettes, recorded snippets—everything that ISN'T the traditional MS Word document with a bullet list of comprehensive points to convey the message. For much of what students want out of life—to call a friend, find their location on GPS, arrange a get-together, create a reminder—writing is passé. Email to your middle school and high school children is as anachronistic as snail mail. Even texting is being shunted aside by vlogs and Skype, and note-taking—with the popularity of apps like Evernote—has become something best accomplished with swipes and clicks.

That's what's killing keyboarding.

But it's not dead yet. Certainly, voice commands can activate a software program or bring up the teacher's website to view homework, but how do you quietly talk to a computer during a lecture? Are programs like Dragon Speak and Siri capable of blocking out extraneous sounds and focusing in on the singular human voice? And don't discount the aesthetics of typing. Take me for example. I'm a K-8 technology teacher. I'm in the know about the latest and greatest in technology trends. I'm expected to try them—and use them. I write for a hobby, but I have arthritis. My doctor wants me to stop typing, switch to Dragon Speak. My modern kids are all for it, but Dragon Speak's quirkiness (like mis-typing oh-so-many words) is distracting. Plus, there's a connection between my brain and fingers that helps me think. Maybe it's as simple as I muse at the speed I type. Maybe the clackity-clack of the keys is soothing to my rattled brain. Nothing in my pedagogic or anecdotal research has convinced me it isn't also true for kids. If we eliminate the peaceful predictability of tapping fingers on those little squares, will getting words on paper be more difficult?

I wonder.

I decided to poll my parents. Overwhelmingly, they support age-appropriate keyboard training for children as young as kindergarten. They understand that typing may be antiquated some day, but not today, or tomorrow. Until it is, they want their kids to learn it.

What do you think?

Photo credit: Beeki (http://pixabay.com/en/cress-spice-plant-keyboard-15086/)

Lesson #7—Halloween Greeting II

Vocabulary	Problem solving	Big Idea
▪ Borders ▪ Clipart ▪ Ctrl ▪ Ctrl+P ▪ Cursor ▪ Drill down ▪ Home row ▪ Insert ▪ Menu bar ▪ My documents ▪ Rubric ▪ Save as ▪ Task bar ▪ Tool bar ▪ Visual	▪ *What's the date? (hover over clock)* ▪ *What's the difference between save and 'save-as'?* ▪ *When do I backspace, when delete?* ▪ *I can't find my story (where did you save it last week?)* ▪ *I don't know where I saved my story (Search from Start button)* ▪ *Why triple click? (to select sentence)* ▪ *Where's 'font color'? (Remember skills from Number Square)* ▪ *My picture went in the wrong spot (did you mark spot with cursor?)* ▪ *Why can't I highlight word to change font (you can—clicking once is faster)*	*Students can use computers to communicate ideas with a multi-media approach*
Time Required *45 minutes*	**NETS-S Standards** *1b, 2b*	**CCSS** *CCSS.ELA-Literacy.W.2.6*

Essential Question
Can color and visual help me share ideas?

Overview

Materials

Internet, MS Word or other word processing program, printer, keyboarding program

Teacher Preparation

- Talk with classroom teacher so you tie story into their writing conversations
- Do students have Word Study? Know what their words are
- Is class shorter than 45 minutes? Highlight items most important to your integration with core classroom studies and leave the rest for 'later'

Steps

_____This is the final week of Word story project. Open project (drill down to file folder on network). If not there, check 'My Documents' or show students how to search.

_____This week, students decorate story to fit theme. Discuss how color and visual can communicate ideas as well as words.

_____Triple-click title (to select a sentence); change to WordArt so it stands out (see inset).

_____In body of story, change color for 3 words by clicking inside word and going to 'font color' tool; match color to word, i.e. make 'pumpkin' orange.

_____Add art border that fits the holiday either from Page Borders or Clip Art.

_____Change font size for three words by clicking inside word and going to 'font size' tool; i.e. make 'guess' font size 72 (to make it emphatic).

_____Change font for three words by clicking inside word and going to 'font' tool; i.e. use 'Chiller' for 'haunted house'.

_____Add three pictures by clicking where pictures belong. Show students the blinking cursor that marks insertion point. Resize as needed.

_____Show students how to see if story fits one page by checking bottom right corner. If story is more than one page, resize font/ images.

_____Check rubric (see end of lesson) to ensure project has required elements.

_____Save with or without assistance with student last name and project name (why student name?); print (Ctrl+P, File-print).

_____Ask students: What digital tools are used in this project? (Hint: software, printer). What else could be used? (Hint: online images, email, pdf). How would they create this story without digital tools? What do they think of that?

_____As you teach, incorporate lesson vocabulary. Check this line if you did that today!

_____Continually throughout class, check for understanding. Expect students to solve problems as they maneuver through lesson and make decisions that follow class rules.

_____Remind students to transfer knowledge to classroom or home.

_____Tuck chairs under desk, headphones over tower; leave station as it was.

Assessment Strategies
- *Remembered earlier skills*
- *Completed project, rubric*
- *Saved to digital portfolio*
- *Followed Common Core and class writing conventions*
- *Understood how digital tools make project possible*

Trouble-shooting:
- *Hardware problems? Have students try to solve before you provide assistance.*
- *Sometimes you need more than one week for a lesson. No worries. There are 32 lessons in text, 35ish in school year. Feel free to stretch a lesson a week or more.*
- *You have print book and need website? Pick grade level and search (Alt+F) name on https://askatechteacher.wordpress.com/great-websites-for-kids/.*

Extension:
- *Students work in pairs to edit their stories.*
- *Publish stories via pdf to class website so students can share with parents.*
- *Show students how to search Google images. Find a picture that fits their story; copy-paste where cursor is blinking.*

- *Extend conversation about visual communication by discussing body language. Show how people are 'read' by their facial expressions, hand movements, body movements—without them saying a word.*
- *Practice keyboarding using installed software or online site.*
- *If students have word study, practice on SpellingCity.com.*
- *Offer additional websites for students to access that tie into class conversations.*
- *If this lesson doesn't work for your students, use one from **How to Jumpstart the Inquiry-based Classroom.** It has 5 projects aligned with SL curriculum.*

More Information:
- *Review "18 Techie Problems Every Student Can Fix" (see end of lesson). Cover these throughout the school year. Expect students to handle these issues.*
- *Lesson questions? Go to http://askatechteacher.com*
- *Second grade teaching wiki: http://smaatechk-3.wikispaces.com/This+Week+in+Tech—Second+Grade*
- *PDF: See appendix for bonus websites*
- *Follow keyboard lessons in K-8 Keyboard Curriculum (http://ow.ly/j6GH8)*

If you don't get through everything, check completed items so you know what to get back to when you have time on later lessons. I find as I focus on the central idea of a lesson, clarifying questions sometimes take more time than I'd expect. I'm fine with that. There'll be lessons later that move faster than I planned.

Name
Teacher
date

HALLOWEEN

Once there was a ghost , a cat and a pumpkin .

They lived in a haunted house . Guess what their favorite holiday was?

Name_____

Teacher's Name_____

HALLOWEEN REBUS
GRADING RUBRIC—2nd GRADE

1. Heading with name, date, teacher   _____
2. A WordArt title, centered   _____
3. Several lines of story   _____
    a. 3 different fonts   _____
    b. 3 different size fonts   _____
    c. 3 different colors   _____
    d. Spell-check   _____
    e. Grammar-check   _____
4. 3 inline pictures—all the same size   _____
5. A festive border   _____
6. Story fills one page but not more   _____
    a. Check Print Preview   _____
7. Professional appearance   _____

Q: How do you make a witch stew?
A: Keep her waiting for hours.

18 Techie Problems Every Student Can Fix

Amazingly, there are twenty tech problems that cause about eighty percent of the stoppages. In the next two pages, I'm going to tell you what those are and how to solve them. Trust me. They're easier than you think. I routinely teach them to third, fourth and fifth graders, and then they teach their parents.

I'll first tell you problem, why it occurs, and finally, the most common solution to fix it:

Deleted a file
Why? By accident or changed my mind
What to do: Open Recycle Bin; right-click—restore

Can't exit a program
Why: Can't find X or Quit tool. This happens with pesky internet ads marketers don't want you to exit
What to do: Alt+F4 works 95% of the time. Try that.

Can't find Word
Why: Shortcut moved, was deleted by accident or became inactive
What to do: Right-click on desktop—select 'New'—"Word Document". Or, use 'search' on Start

Keyboard doesn't work
Why: Lost connection
What to do: First check to be sure it actually isn't working by pushing 'Num Lock'. If the 'Num Lock'

light go on/off, the problem is not the keyboard. If it does: Re-plug cord into back of tower or reboot

Mouse doesn't work
Why: Lost connection
What to do: Move it around to see if the cursor moves. If it doesn't, re-plug cord into back or reboot

Start button is gone
Why: Task bar disappeared
What to do: Push Flying Windows (lower right corner of keyboard)

No sound
Why: Mute is on; volume is down; headphones are unplugged
What to do: Unmute the sound or turn it up; plug headphones in; reboot

Do you notice how often I say reboot? Sometimes, the computer simply gets confused and drops actions out of the queue which means they stop working. All you have to do is restart the system to get things back to normal.

Can't find a file
Why: Saved wrong, moved

What to do: Push Start button—Start search; when you find it, resave in a location you will remember

Menu command grayed out

Why: You're in another command

What to do: Push escape 3 times. This d makes the command you'd like to use available

What's today's date?

Why: You forgot!

What to do: Hover over clock; in Word, use the shortkey Shift+Alt+D

Taskbar was moved

Why: Student interference

What to do: Click on an open part of taskbar; drag to bottom of screen (or where you prefer it to be)

Desktop icons messed up

Why: Student interference; you added more icons and now everything's confused

What to do: Right click on screen—select 'Sort by', select method you'd like icons arranged

Computer frozen

Why: Mouse frozen; keyboard frozen, dialogue box open

What to do: Check solutions in this list. If nothing works, reboot

Program frozen

Why: Dialog box open; not selected on taskbar

What to do: Look around screen for dialogue box wanting input. Answer. Or click program on taskbar

I erased my document/text

Why: Ooops

What to do: Ctrl+Z

Screen says "Ctrl-Alt-Del"

Why: You rebooted

What to do: Hold down Ct+Alt—then push Delete. This will bring you to log-in screen or desktop

Program closed down

Why: Ooops

What to do: If on taskbar, click. If not, reopen—see if right sidebar shows a back-up and open that

Tool bar missing at top of www

Why: Unknown

What to do: Push F11 key

Lesson #8—Reading on the Internet

Vocabulary	Problem solving	Big Idea
▨ *Address bar* ▨ *Back button* ▨ *Bling* ▨ *Browser* ▨ *Desktop* ▨ *Escape* ▨ *Hand* ▨ *Internet neighborhood* ▨ *Internet Explorer* ▨ *Internet start page* ▨ *Scroll* ▨ *Search bar* ▨ *Search engine* ▨ *Tool bar*	▨ *Program's gone (check taskbar)* ▨ *What if I don't like webpage I'm on (use back key or class internet start page tab)* ▨ *Webpage text is too small (Ctrl++ to zoom in)* ▨ *I clicked X, but internet didn't close (is a dialogue box open that says 'close all tabs'?)* ▨ *I clicked on bling! (use back arrow to get out)* ▨ *I can't find link (where cursor becomes a hand)*	*Reading on the computer enables connections that print books don't*
Time Required *45 minutes*	**NETS-S Standards** *3b*	**CCSS** *CCSS.ELA-Literacy.RF.2.4*

Essential Question
How do I use technology to read?

Overview

Materials

Internet, story websites, iPads (if using these), keyboarding program

Teacher Preparation

- Talk with classroom teacher so you tie into their inquiry
- Have a list of story websites on class internet start page
- Have internet safety websites on start page
- Is your class shorter than 45 minutes? Highlight items most important to your integration with core classroom studies and leave the rest for 'later'.

Steps

_____Warm up by keyboarding home row with an online site like DanceMat Typing or Nimble Fingers (Google names for addresses):

- *hands in home row position, curved over keys*
- *posture—body centered in front of keyboard, legs in front of body*
- *technique—use finger closest to required key; control flying fingers/hands*

_____Done? Before students read a story from internet, discuss internet neighborhood. How should they stay safe in this unknown world? (see flier at end of lesson):

- *Stay on assigned link*
- *If you get off of it, use back arrow or start page tab*
- *Only go to websites teacher has approved*
- *Don't talk to strangers*

_____Watch these two videos on safe internet use (Google for addresses):

- *BrainPop Jr—Internet Safety*
- *My Online Neighborhood*

_____Want more before starting internet use? Watch this internet safety video http://www.youtube.com/watch?v=89eCHtFs0XM&feature=youtu.be.

_____Model how to 1) access internet, 2) find class start page, and 3) go to links being used today. Point out ads to be avoided. Point out bling.

_____Today, we read. What can you do on an internet story you can't do on a book story? (Answers: click links for enrichments, take a pile of books wherever you go, not worry about ripping pages—anything else?).

_____Open browser—what's a 'browser'? How does it help students find websites?

_____Select a story from class list (see examples at end of lesson). Take students on a tour—tool bars, links, 'hand' that identifies link, back/forward button, home tool, address bar, browser tabs. Clarify where they can go on a site and where they can't (i.e., ads, any link out of teacher-provided one).

_____Use tabs on browser to move between class internet start page and approved links.

_____Now set students lose to read!

_____When done, students share details of story with neighbor. Show comprehension of story, plot, characters, and vocabulary. Ask each other for help decoding prefixes and suffixes and unknown words. Follow class rules for conversations (speak one at a time, listen to each other with care, gain floor in respectful ways--as outlined in CCSS.ELA-Literacy.SL.2.1a).

_____As you teach, incorporate lesson vocabulary. Check this line if you did that today!

_____Throughout class, check for understanding. Expect students to solve problems and make decisions that follow class rules.

_____Remind students to transfer this knowledge to the classroom or home.

Assessment Strategies
- *Anecdotal observation*
- *Transferred knowledge*
- *Shared understanding of story with classmate*

_____Close to desktop. Tuck chairs under desk, headphones over tower; leave station as it was.

Trouble-shooting:
- *Student hears sounds not from story they are reading? Close tab it's coming from.*
- *Hardware problems? Have students try to solve them before providing assistance.*
- *Sometimes you need more than one week for a lesson. No worries. There are 32 lessons in text, 35ish in school year. Feel free to stretch a lesson a week or more.*

- *You have print book and need website? Pick grade level and search (Alt+F) name on https://askatechteacher.wordpress.com/great-websites-for-kids/.*

Extension:

- *If you have iPads, transfer stories to them. Let students get comfy while reading.*
- *Tie this in with school DEAR program (or Sustained Silent Reading).*
- *Offer inquiry websites for students who have done enough reading (math, etc.).*
- *Replace lesson with Kindergarten lesson #1 Blabberize Me! in curriculum extendors (http://www.structuredlearning.net/book/k-6-curriculum-extender/).*
- *Replace with Kindergarten Lesson #2 SmartScreen Read-aloud in curriculum extendors (http://www.structuredlearning.net/book/k-6-curriculum-extender/).*
- *Replace with Third Grade Lesson #2 Puzzle Maker to Prepare for Tests in curriculum extendors (http://www.structuredlearning.net/book/k-6-curriculum-extender/).*

More Information:

- *Lesson questions? Go to http://askatechteacher.com*
- *Second grade teaching wiki:*
  http://smaatechk-3.wikispaces.com/This+Week+in+Tech—Second+Grade
- *PDF: See appendix for bonus websites*
- *Follow keyboard lessons in K-8 Keyboard Curriculum (http://ow.ly/j6GH8)*

If you don't get through everything, check completed items so you know what to get back to when you have time on later lessons. I find as I focus on the central idea of a lesson, clarifying questions sometimes take more time than I'd expect. I'm fine with that. There'll be lessons later that move faster than I planned.

PDF extra: Links to story websites

If you have a print book, go to http://askatechteacher, Great Websites, 2nd grade, stories

1.	Aesop's Fables	14.	Make your story a newspaper
2.	Aesop Fables—no ads	15.	Mighty Book
3.	Badguy Patrol	16.	Stories—MeeGenius
4.	Childhood Stories	17.	Stories to read from PBS kids
5.	Classic Fairy Tales	18.	Stories to read—Int'l Library
6.	Edutainment stories	19.	Stories—Signed
7.	Fairy Tales and Fables	20.	Stories for youngsters
8.	Fables—beautiful	21.	Stories to read — Starfall
9.	Interactive stories	22.	Storybook Maker
10.	Free non-fic audio books	23.	Storytime for me
11.	Make another story	24.	Web-based Madlibs
12.	Make Your Story	25.	Zooburst—pop up stories
13.	Make Believe Comix		

Don't talk to strangers. Look both ways before crossing the (virtual) street. Don't go places you don't know. Play fair. Pick carefully who you trust. Don't get distracted by bling. And sometimes, stop everything and take a nap.

Lesson #9—Holiday Letter in Word I

Vocabulary	Problem solving	Big Idea
▪ *Alignment* ▪ *Body* ▪ *Closing* ▪ *Fonts* ▪ *Format* ▪ *Heading* ▪ *Icon* ▪ *Print preview* ▪ *Red /green squiggles* ▪ *Shift* ▪ *Tool* ▪ *Tool bar* ▪ *Wrap*	▪ *Caps stuck (is caps lock on?)* ▪ *How do I log on (do you know user name and password?)* ▪ *What's today's date? (hover over clock)* ▪ *I can't find my letter (search)* ▪ *Which alignment tool is center (hover over tools)* ▪ *What's the difference between grammar and formatting?* ▪ *What's the difference between save and 'save-as'?*	*Use technology to improve letter-writing skills*
Time Required *45 minutes*	**NETS-S Standards** *2a, 6a*	**CCSS** *CCSS.ELA-Literacy.W.2.5*

Essential Question
How do I use technology to write a letter?

Overview

Materials

Internet, word processing program, spelling words, rubrics

Teacher Preparation

- This two-week project (Lesson 9/10) can be flipped with Lesson 11, depending upon timing of holiday
- Talk with classroom teacher to find out which grammar rules they are discussing
- Know student spelling words for the week
- Post websites related to topics being discussed in class on internet start page
- Is class shorter than 45 minutes? Highlight items most important to your integration with core classroom studies and leave the rest for 'later'.

Steps

_____This is a two-week project in word processing, to teach formatting skills while reinforcing classroom study on grammar, spelling and elements of a letter.

_____Open word processing program (Word, Google Docs, Open Office or similar) as independently as possible.

_____Type heading (name, teacher, date—enter between each line). Explain alignment, that this is left aligned. Show Word's alignment tools.

_____Discuss letter writing skills students have learned in class, like:

- *write a letter*
- *describe actions, thoughts, and feelings where required*
- *use temporal words to signal event order where required*

_____Type a letter to parents about why students are thankful. Use font size 14-16. Adjust font look as learned in Lesson 7. Remind students text wraps to next line—no need to push enter. See samples on next page.

_____As students type, reinforce keyboarding skills such as elbows at sides, hands on homerow, legs in front of body. Remind students: Every time they use computer, practice good habits.

_____Check grammar/spelling; clear red/green squiggles.

_____Done? Work with neighbor to strengthen writing by adding details, clarifying issues.

_____Continually throughout class, check for understanding. Expect students to solve problems as they maneuver through lesson and make decisions that follow class rules.

_____As you teach, incorporate lesson vocab. Check this line item if you did that today!

_____Letter must be one page. Show students how to check if they have accomplished this goal.

_____Save (or should they 'save-as'?) with last name in file name (why?). Tuck chairs under desk, headphones over tower; leave station as you found it.

Assessment Strategies
- *Saved to network folder*
- *Used knowledge learned in prior lessons*
- *Worked well with neighbor*
- *Strengthened story by revising and editing*
- *Transferred knowledge to other classes/everyday life*
- *Practiced writing conventions from class and highlighted in Common Core*

Trouble-shooting:
- *Hardware problems? Have students try to solve them before providing assistance.*
- *Sometimes you need more than one week for a lesson. No worries. There are 32 lessons in text, 35ish in school year. Feel free to stretch a lesson a week or more.*
- *You have print book and need website link? Pick the grade level and search name on this website https://askatechteacher.wordpress.com/great-websites-for-kids/.*

Extension:
- *Students who finish: Practice spelling words on SpellingCity.com.*
- *Students who finish: Visit internet start page for websites that go with classwork.*
- *Replace this lesson with 1st Grade lesson #5 I Am a Puzzle in curriculum extendors (http://www.structuredlearning.net/book/k-6-curriculum-extender/).*
- *Replace this lesson with 4th Grade Lesson #4 Book Review in curriculum extendors (http://www.structuredlearning.net/book/k-6-curriculum-extender/).*

More Information:
- *Lesson questions? Go to http://askatechteacher.com*
- *Second grade teaching wiki:*

http://smaatechk-3.wikispaces.com/This+Week+in+Tech—Second+Grade
- *PDF: See appendix for bonus websites*
- *Follow keyboard lessons in K-8 Keyboard Curriculum (http://ow.ly/j6GH8)*

If you don't get through everything, check completed items so you know what to get back to when you have time. Clarifying questions sometimes take more time than expected. Be fine with that. There'll be lessons later that move faster than I planned.

Samples letters students—three levels of mastery

Lesson #10—Holiday Letter in Word II

Vocabulary	Problem solving	Big Idea
 ▪ Clipart ▪ Ctrl+Z ▪ Handles ▪ Image ▪ Protocol ▪ Resize ▪ Rubric ▪ Save as ▪ Start button ▪ Taskbar ▪ Undo ▪ Windows	▪ Double-click doesn't work? (push enter) ▪ Deleted letter by accident (Ctrl+Z) ▪ I messed up my letter (Ctrl+Z) ▪ How do I close Word? (Alt+F4) ▪ How do I change word color? (click inside word; pick color) ▪ What's the difference between save and 'save as'? ▪ What's the difference between backspace and delete? ▪ How do I clear red and green squiggly lines?	*Use technology to improve letter-writing skills*

Time Required	NETS-S Standards	CCSS
45 minutes	*2a, 6a*	*CCSS.ELA-Literacy.W.2.6*

Essential Question
How do I use technology to write a letter?

Overview

Materials

Internet, word processing program, printer, rubric, keyboarding program

Teacher Preparation

- This two-week project (Lesson 9/10) can be flipped with Lesson 11, depending upon timing of holidays
- Talk with class teacher about grammar rules and letter writing being discussed in class
- Post websites on class inquiry on class internet start page
- Is class shorter than 45 minutes? Highlight items most important to your integration with core classroom studies and leave the rest for 'later'.

Steps

_____This is second of two-week MS Word project (or another word processing program) to teach formatting skills as well as reinforce classroom study on grammar, spelling and elements of a letter.

_____Open student letter started last week as independently as possible.

_____Can't find it? Check 'My Documents'—student may have saved it wrong. If not there, show student how to search using their last name.

_____Review writing conventions.

_____Click inside a word; change font color, font look, and font size (as done before).

_____Add three pictures to body of letter (not heading or closing) using clip art as learned in Lesson 7. Resize as needed so letter fits one page. See inset for example.

_____Remind students: Every time they use computer, practice good habits.

_____Add festive border.

_____Show students how to check page count to see if letters fits one page. Adjust font and picture sizes as needed.

_____As you teach, incorporate lesson vocabulary. Check this line if you did that today!

_____Continually throughout class, check for understanding. Expect students to make decisions that follow class rules.

_____Check rubric at end of Lesson to be sure all required elements are included. Students submit rubric with printed letter.

_____Save and print without assistance. Should students save or save-as?

_____Remind students to transfer knowledge to the classroom or home.

_____Leave station as it was (chairs in, desktop clean, headphones over tower, textbook behind monitor).

Assessment Strategies

- *Completed project, rubric*
- *Used knowledge from prior lessons*
- *Transferred knowledge to other classes/everyday life*
- *Understood digital tools*

Trouble-shooting:

- *Made a mistake (deleted by accident, did something you have no clue how)? Ctrl+Z until back where student likes it (see poster at end of lesson).*
- *Sometimes you need more than one week for a lesson. No worries. There are 32 lessons in text, 35ish in school year. Feel free to stretch a lesson a week or more.*
- *You have print book and need website? Pick grade level and search (Alt+F) name on https://askatechteacher.wordpress.com/great-websites-for-kids/.*

Extension:

- *Students can work in pairs to fill out rubric, helping each other.*
- *Those who finish: Practice keyboarding on installed software or online keyboarding*
- *If this lesson doesn't work for your students, use one from **How to Jumpstart the Inquiry-based Classroom.** It has 5 projects aligned with SL curriculum.*

More Information:

- *Lesson questions? Go to http://askatechteacher.com*
- *Second grade teaching wiki: http://smaatechk-3.wikispaces.com/This+Week+in+Tech—Second+Grade*
- *PDF: See appendix for bonus websites*
- *Follow keyboard lessons in K-8 Keyboard Curriculum (http://ow.ly/j6GH8)*

If you don't get through everything, check completed items so you know what to get back to when you have time on later lessons. I find as I focus on the central idea of a lesson, clarifying questions sometimes take more time than I'd expect. I'm fine with that. There'll be lessons later that move faster than I planned.

*Name*_____

*Teacher's Name*_____

LETTER WRITING RUBRIC
2nd Grade

1. Heading with name, date, teacher   _____

2. Greeting   _____

3. Closing   _____

4. Several lines of a letter   _____

     a. Different fonts   _____

     b. Different size fonts   _____

     c. Different colors   _____

     d. Spell-check   _____

     e. Grammar-check   _____

5. Inline pictures—all the same size   _____

6. A festive border   _____

7. Story fills one page but not more   _____

8. Professional appearance   _____

UNDO

is your Friend

Lesson #11—Graphic Organizers

Vocabulary	Problem solving	Big Idea
🖳 *Clipart* 🖳 *Diagram* 🖳 *Doc* 🖳 *Formatting* 🖳 *Graphic organizer* 🖳 *Heading* 🖳 *Print preview* 🖳 *Ribbon* 🖳 *SmartArt* 🖳 *Visual learning* 🖳 *Visual organizer*	🖳 *Program disappeared (check taskbar)* 🖳 *I can't close program (Alt+F4)* 🖳 *My computer doesn't work (wake mouse up, check power)* 🖳 *I can't find Diagram Toolbar (click on diagram)* 🖳 *My project takes two pages* 🖳 *My graphic organizer is on top of title (drag it down)*	*Share information visually—as a picture—to make it more exciting and clearer*
Time Required *45 minutes*	**NETS-S Standards** *2c, 3b*	**CCSS** *CCSS.ELA-Literacy.W.2.6*

Essential Question

How can I communicate information quickly and clearly?

Overview

Materials

Internet, MS Word, keyboard program, alternate graphic organizers (if desired)

Teacher Preparation

- Talk with classroom teacher so you tie visual organizer into their conversations
- See if math class is discussing set theory; tie into that with pyramid construction
- Post websites on internet start page that support class inquiry
- Is class shorter than 45 minutes? Highlight items most important to your integration with core classroom studies and leave the rest for 'later'

Steps

_____This is the last project in MS Word/word processing unit. After this, expect students to be able to use this program with nominal assistance for class projects.

_____Every year starting in second grade, students create a project that communicates an idea using visual organizers. This is it.

_____What is a visual organizer (graphic organizer)? How does it help to communicate information (by displaying information in a picture format)? How does it facilitate sharing? Show students examples from last year's 2nd, 3rd, 4th grade classes. Is information clear? Do they understand the message?

_____This project supports a classroom conversation and can be done in various word processing programs, i.e., Open Office, Google Docs. We use MS Word. Visual organizer can be from various online sites (see extensions). We use Word's SmartArt.

_____Demonstrate (see inset): Open Word; add heading. Why heading?

_____Add title (*How I'm Organized*) font size 16, centered and bold. Push enter so graphic organizer will appear underneath.

_____Insert SmartArt. Word offers many—choose one that works for your student group. Once you've selected it, add shapes to get six (or number you need for your topic).

_____Add text to each layer as fits topic.

_____Format with 'change colors' and 'SmartArt Styles'

_____Add student name at pinnacle with WordArt

_____Use 'print preview' to be sure all information appears on one page. If not, resize as needed and print.

_____Save to network; save-as to flash drive (if available). What's the difference between save and 'save-as'? Why include student last name in file name?

_____When students finished, ask them what digital tools were used today (Hint: software, internet, online tools, printer).

_____Continually throughout class, check for understanding. Expect students to solve problems as they make decisions that follow class rules.

_____Remind students to transfer knowledge to classroom or home.

_____As you teach, incorporate lesson vocabulary. Check this line if you did that today!

_____When students finish, practice keyboarding using online website that focuses on one row at a time (i.e., DanceMat Typing, Nimble Fingers). This month: Concentrate on QWERTY row. Watch posture. Keep hands on keyboard. Use finger closest to key.

_____Close program (with Alt+F4).

_____Tuck chairs under desk, headphones over tower; leave station as you found it.

Assessment Strategies

- *Anecdotal observation*
- *Saved to digital portfolio*
- *Completed project*
- *Used prior knowledge*
- *Joined class conversation*
- *Understood digital tools used*

Trouble-shooting:

- *There's not enough room to type what student needs to? Resize font.*
- *There's still not enough room? Students should evaluate what they've written, edit it to be as concise as possible. How can they say more in less words?*
- *There's still not enough room (summarize information).*
- *Occasionally when students have difficulty doing what you are teaching, ask why. And listen. You may be surprised by the answer.*
- *You have print book and need website? Pick grade level and search (Alt+F) name on https://askatechteacher.wordpress.com/great-websites-for-kids/.*

- *Sometimes you need more than one week for a lesson. No worries. There are 32 lessons in text, 35ish in school year. Feel free to stretch a lesson a week or more.*

Extension:
- *Add pictures of events in a row at top or bottom (see sample at end of lesson); resize so they are consistent and fit in one row.*
- *If brevity and word choice is a concern in your classroom, consider creating a class Twitter stream. Students will want to participate and will be forced to keep their entries to 140 characters. See the article at end of lesson for Twitter in the classroom ideas.*
- *Find lots of graphic organizers for free online (PDF owners: click these bonus websites for additional resources):*

  - *Graphic organizers*
  - *Graphic organizers II*
  - *Graphic Organizers III*
  - *Graphic organizers—all topics*
  - *Graphic organizers—Enchanted Learning*
  - *Graphic Organizers—for reading*

- *Offer additional websites for students who are done reading (math, etc.).*
- *Replace this lesson with 4th Grade Lesson #5 iPads 101 in curriculum extendors (http://www.structuredlearning.net/book/k-6-curriculum-extender/).*
- *Offer websites that tie into class conversation.*

More Information:
- *Lesson questions? Go to http://askatechteacher.com*
- *Second grade teaching wiki:*
  http://smaatechk-3.wikispaces.com/This+Week+in+Tech—Second+Grade
- *PDF: See appendix for bonus websites*
- *Follow keyboard lessons in K-8 Keyboard Curriculum (http://ow.ly/j6GH8)*

If you don't get through everything, check completed items so you know what to get back to when you have time on later lessons. I find as I focus on the central idea of a lesson, clarifying questions sometimes take more time than I'd expect. I'm fine with that. There'll be lessons later that move faster than I planned.

Computer: a device designed to speed and automate errors.

HOW I'M ORGANIZED

Your name
Your Teacher
Date

HOW I'M ORGANIZED

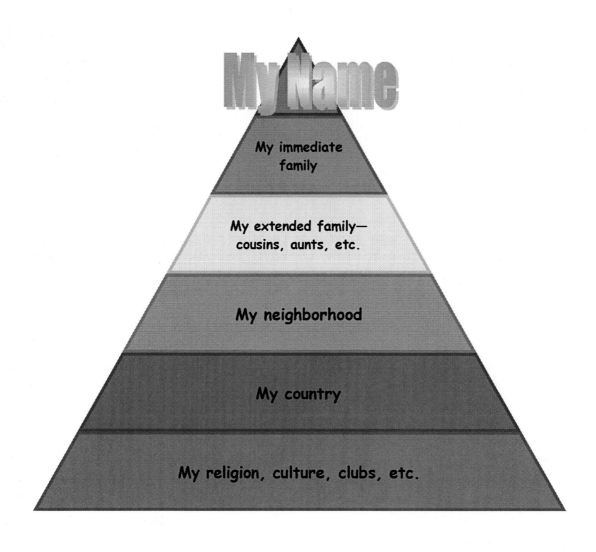

My Name

My immediate family

My extended family—cousins, aunts, etc.

My neighborhood

My country

My religion, culture, clubs, etc.

13 ways Twitter Improves Education

A teachers challenge is to communicate with students in a way they will hear her/him. Twitter might be perfect for your class.

Twitter can easily be dismissed as a waste of time in the elementary school classroom. Students get distracted. They might see inappropriate tweets. How does a teacher manage a room full of Tweeple?

But, you've read a lot about Twitters usefulness in writing skills and sharing information so you—of the Open Minded Attitude—want to try it. Here's ammunition for what often turns into a pitched, take-sides verbal brawl as well-intended educators try to reach a compromise on using Twitter (in fact, many Web 2.0 tools--blogs, wikis, discussion forums, and websites that require registrations and log-ins--can be added to the list) that works for all stakeholders:

You learn to be concise

Twitter gives you only 140 characters to get the entire message across. *Letters, numbers, symbols, punctuation and spaces all count as characters on Twitter.* Wordiness doesn't work. Twitter counts every keystroke and won't publish anything with a minus in front of the word count.

At first blush, that seems impossible. It's not. It challenges students to know the right word for every situation. People with a big vocabulary are at an advantage because they don't use collections of little words to say what they mean. All those hints from English teachers about picture nouns and action verbs and getting rid of adverbs and adjectives take on new importance to the Twitter aficionado.

Twitter isn't intimidating

A blank white page that holds hundreds of words, demanding you fill in each line margin to margin is intimidating. 140 characters isn't. Anyone can write 140 characters about a topic. Students write their 140 characters and more, learn to whittle back, leave out emotional words, adjectives and adverbs, pick better nouns and verbs because they need the room. Instead of worrying what to say on all those empty lines, they feel successful.

Students learn manners

Social networks are all about netiquette. People thank others for their assistance, ask politely for help, encourage contributions from others. Use this framework to teach students how to engage in a community--be it physical or virtual. It's all about manners.

Students learn to focus

With only 140 characters, you can't get off topic or cover tangential ideas. You have to save those for a different tweet. Tweeple like that trait in writers. They like to hear the writer's thoughts on the main topic, not meanderings. When forced to write this way, students will find it doesn't take a paragraph to make a point. Use the right words, people get it. Consider that the average reader gives a story seven seconds before moving on. OK, yes, that's more than 140 characters, but not much.

Here's an idea: If you feel you must get into those off-topic thoughts. write them in a separate tweet.

Students learn to share
Start a tweet stream where students share research on a topic. Maybe it's Ancient Greece. Have each student share their favorite website (using a #hashtag -- maybe #ancientgreece) and you've created a resource others can use. Expand on that wonderful skill learned in kindergarten about sharing personal toys. Encourage students to RT (retweet) posts they found particularly relevant or helpful.

Writing short messages perfects the art of "headlining"
Writers call this the title. Bloggers and journalists call it the headline. Whatever the label, it has to be cogent and pithy enough to pull the audience in and make them read the article. That's a tweet.

Tweets need to be written knowing that tweeple can @reply
Yes. This is a world of social networks where people read what you say and comment. That's a good thing. It's feedback and builds an online community, be it for socializing or school. Students learn to construct their arguments expecting others to respond, question, comment. Not only does this develop the skill of persuasive writing, students learn to have a thick skin, take comments with a grain of salt and two grains of aspirin.

#Hashtags develop a community
Create #hashtags that will help students organize their tweets--#help if they have a question, #homework for homework help. Establish class hashtags to deal with subjects you want students to address.

Students learn tolerance for all opinions
Why? Because Tweeple aren't afraid to voice their thoughts. They only have 140 characters—so they spit it right out. Because the Twitter stream is a public forum (in a classroom, the stream can be private, visible to only class members), students understand what they say is out there forever. That's daunting. Take the opportunity to teach students about their public profile. Represent themselves well with good grammar, good spelling, well-chosen tolerant ideas. Don't be emotional or spiteful because it can't be taken back. Rather than shying away from exposing students to the world, use Twitter to teach students how to live in it.

Breaks down barriers to talking to other people

Students are less worried about typing 140 characters than raising their hand in class, all eyes on them, and having to spit out the right answer. With Twitter, students can type an answer, delete it, edit it, add to and detract from, all before they push send. Plus, it's more anonymous than the class, with no body language or facial expressions. Just words--and not many of those. Students have their say, see how others respond, have a chance to clarify. What could be safer?

Students are engaged

Twitter is exciting, new, hip. Students want to use it. It's not the boring worksheet. It's a way to engage students in ways that excite them.

Consider this: You're doing the lecture part of teaching (we all have some of that), or you're walking the classroom helping where needed. Students can tweet questions that show up on the Smartboard. It's easy to see where everyone is getting stuck, which question is stumping them, and answer it in real time. The class barely slows down. Not only can you see where problems arise, students can provide instant feedback on material without disrupting class. Three people can tweet at once while you talk/help.

Twitter, the Classroom Notepad

I tried this out after I read about it on my PLN. Springboarding off student engagement, Twitter can act as your classroom notepad. Have students enter their thoughts, note, reactions while you talk. By the time class is done, the entire class has an overview of the conversation with extensions and connections that help everyone get more out of the inquiry.

Twitter is always open

Inspiration doesn't always strike in that 50-minute class period. Sometimes it's after class, after school, after dinner, even 11 at night. Twitter doesn't care. Whatever schedule is best for students to discover the answer, Twitter is there. If you post a tweet question and ask students to join the conversation, they will respond in the time frame that works best for them. That's a new set of rules for classroom participation, and these are student-centered, uninhibited by a subjective time period. Twitter doesn't even care if a student missed class. S/he can catch up via tweets and then join in.

Lesson #12—Problem Solving

Vocabulary	Problem solving	Big Idea
Alt Challenge Ctrl Flying windows Keyboard shortcuts Password PW Shortkeys Start button Task bar UN User name	I lost my work (Ctrl+Z—undo—or check taskbar at bottom of screen) I can't close a program (Alt+F4) I can't save (Ctrl+S) I can't find the tool (use shortkey) I can't print (did you print to class printer or somewhere else?) Computer didn't save (did you save to network?) Computer lost part of my project (check folder for more recent save)	*Problem-solving in technology usually involves common sense and doing what worked in the past*
Time Required 45 minutes	**NETS-S Standards** 4a, 4b	**CCSS** CCSS.ELA-Literacy

Essential Question
How do I use technology when there are so many problems?

Overview

Materials

Copies of Problem Solving Challenge for students, prizes (if using them), holiday website list, problem solving board

Teacher Preparation

- Talk with class teacher. Are students experiencing recurring problems on class computers? Favorites: 'Can't print' and 'save didn't work'
- Be sure class problem solving board is up to date (see inset)
- Is class shorter than 45 minutes? Highlight items most important to your integration with core classroom studies and leave the rest for 'later'

Steps

_____Discuss computer problems with students. Start with a review of hardware-based problems. Challenge students to see who knows these:

- *Volume doesn't work—are headphones plugged in? Is volume on?*
- *Computer doesn't work—is power on?*
- *Mouse doesn't work—is light on*
- *Monitor doesn't work—is power on?*

_____What problems have you noticed during class this year? Cover those with students and solicit their solutions.

_____What problems do students run into when they use computers at home or in class? Write them on SmartScreen as students list them:

- *What's user name? What's password?*
- *I can't exit the program (Alt+F4)*
- *Start button disappeared (push 'flying windows' button)*
- *I lost my work (Ctrl+Z)*
- *Program shut down (Is it on task bar?)*

_____Discuss problem solving strategies:

- *What has worked in the past?*
- *Look around screen to see if there's a solution.*
- *Be a risk taker! Don't be afraid to try things.*
- *How far can you go without asking for help?*

_____Today, students will play Problem Solving Challenge. Pass out copies of common problems your student group faces or use the one in this book (it may cover yours). This list can also include hardware problems (see list above) and shortkeys (see Lesson 2).

_____Divide class into groups. Give ten minutes to study problem solving list. Collect papers.

_____If there is an extra student, make them time keeper.

_____Go to Group One. Present them with a problem. Give them five seconds to solve and then move onto next group. Give that group five seconds and so on until solution is revealed or all groups had a chance. If no one answers, provide the answer.

_____Go to Group Two and ask them to solve next problem. Repeat process from above.

_____Each right answer gets one point.

_____Make note of where groups have difficulties so you can cover them in the future.

_____Continue until you run out of time.

_____Prizes? Optional. I give Free passes (see inset) that include sitting where student wants, skip a homework, extra credit—prizes I know they value and will get them excited. You might decide to have no prizes.

Assessment Strategies
- Anecdotal observation
- Able to solve problems

_____As you teach, incorporate lesson vocabulary. Check this line if you did that today!

_____Remind students to transfer knowledge to classroom or home.

_____Tuck chairs under desk; leave station as you found it.

Trouble-shooting:

- Sometimes you need more than one week for a lesson. No worries. There are 32 lessons in text, 35ish in the school year. Feel free to stretch a lesson a week or more.
- You have print book and need website? Pick grade level and search (Alt+F) name on https://askatechteacher.wordpress.com/great-websites-for-kids/.

Extension:
- Put this into a Jeopardy template (see appendix for sites).
- Set up a board where students can post a problem anonymously.
- Keep list of problems students encounter and have them help each other.
- Done? Go to holiday-themed websites like these (Google for addresses):

  - 12 Days of Christmas
  - Penguin Show
  - Reindeer Orchestra
  - NORAD Santa
  - Elf Academy

- Practice keyboarding with online program. Students should only practice the row they are currently working on, i.e., QWERTY or lower row. Remind students to keep elbows at their sides, hands on their own side of keyboard, feet in front of body.
- Replace with Third Grade Lesson #3 Create a Timeline of Events in curriculum extendors (http://www.structuredlearning.net/book/k-6-curriculum-extender/).

More Information:
- Lesson questions? Go to http://askatechteacher.com
- Second grade teaching wiki:
  http://smaatechk-3.wikispaces.com/This+Week+in+Tech—Second+Grade
- PDF: See appendix for bonus websites
- Follow keyboard lessons in K-8 Keyboard Curriculum (http://ow.ly/j6GH8)

If you don't get through everything, check completed items so you know what to get back to when you have time on later lessons. I find as I focus on the central idea of a lesson, clarifying questions sometimes take more time than I'd expect. I'm fine with that. There'll be lessons later that move faster than I planned.

"If it's really a supercomputer, how come the bullets don't bounce off when I shoot it?"

TROUBLESHOOTING COMPUTER PROBLEMS

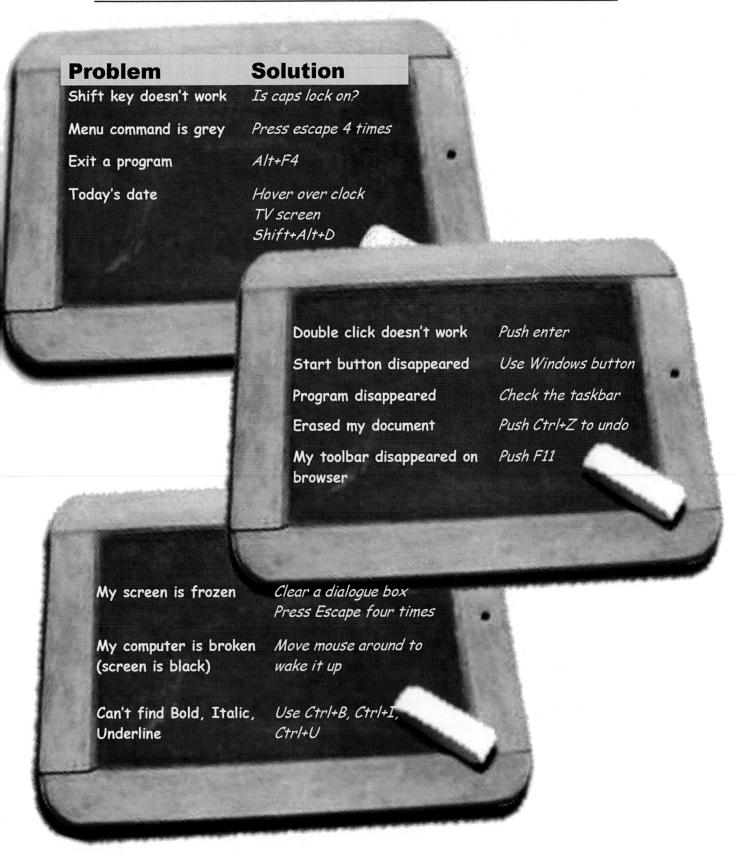

Problem	Solution
Shift key doesn't work	*Is caps lock on?*
Menu command is grey	*Press escape 4 times*
Exit a program	*Alt+F4*
Today's date	*Hover over clock* *TV screen* *Shift+Alt+D*
Double click doesn't work	*Push enter*
Start button disappeared	*Use Windows button*
Program disappeared	*Check the taskbar*
Erased my document	*Push Ctrl+Z to undo*
My toolbar disappeared on browser	*Push F11*
My screen is frozen	*Clear a dialogue box* *Press Escape four times*
My computer is broken (screen is black)	*Move mouse around to wake it up*
Can't find Bold, Italic, Underline	*Use Ctrl+B, Ctrl+I, Ctrl+U*

Lesson #13—Holiday Greetings in Publisher

Vocabulary	Problem solving	Big Idea
Canvas *Desktop publishing* *Flier* *Font* *Graphics* *Greeting cards* *Image* *Online tool* *Scheme* *Software* *Template* *Text box*	*Can't exit program (Alt+F4)* *Document disappeared (check taskbar)* *Can't write on card (insert text box)* *I deleted picture by accident (Ctrl+Z)* *I can't change pages (use left panel)* *How do I print all pages (push print once; they all print)* *I printed—it came out weird (fold)*	*I can share a celebration with technology*

Time Required	NETS-S Standards	CCSS
45 minutes	*1b, 2b*	*CCSS.ELA-Literacy.W.2.6*

Essential Question
What technology is best for sharing holiday greetings?

Overview

Materials

Internet, knowledge of a community service project, desktop publishing software/online tool, required links on class internet start page, printer, keyboarding program

Teacher Preparation

- Can students create cards for a community service project?
- Websites on internet start page that support class inquiry
- Is class shorter than 45 minutes? Highlight the items most important to your integration with core classroom studies and leave the rest for 'later'

Steps

_____Discuss the difference between software and online programs? Can students name a few of each that they have used? Which are digital tools? (Hint: Both—why?)

_____Today we are creating holiday greeting cards using:

- *Kerpoof*
- *Hallmark (or other online card creator)*
- *Publisher*

_____Demo all three. Here, I focus on Publisher because it has the most options and is the most intuitive.

_____Open Publisher. Students used KidPix last year for cards. Compare: tools, toolbars, canvas. Notice how much more sophisticated Publisher is—the card looks real!

_____Walk students through Publisher opening screen—task pane, page layout, middle work area, ribbons, menus.

_____Find 'Greeting Cards', 'Holiday cards'. Click template you like (what's a template?). Select color/font scheme and click 'create'.

_____Review card (text boxes with greetings, pictures, name on back). This year, students only change:

- *pg. 2 (add an image)*
- *pg. 4 (add their name)*

_____Go to page 2 and add holiday picture (through clipart); resize as needed.

_____Go to page 4 and change card creator to student name.

_____Remind students: Every time they use the computer, practice good keyboarding skills.

_____Continually throughout class, check for understanding. Expect students to make decisions that follow class rules.

_____Print card; show students how to fold (top down, side to side, white side in); save with assistance to network. Include student last name in file name (why?).

_____Those who finish: Practice keyboarding on installed software or online websites.

_____As you teach, incorporate lesson vocabulary. Check this line if you did that today!

_____Remind students to transfer knowledge to classroom or home.

_____Tuck chairs under desk; leave station as you found it.

Assessment Strategies

- *Anecdotal observation*
- *Completed project*
- *Understood use of digital tools to produce and share project*

Trouble-shooting:
- *Hardware problems? Have students try to solve before asking for help.*
- *You have print book and need website? Pick grade level and search (Alt+F) name on https://askatechteacher.wordpress.com/great-websites-for-kids/.*
- *Sometimes you need more than one week for a lesson. No worries. There are 32 lessons in text, 35ish in school year. Feel free to stretch a lesson a week or more.*

Extension:
- *Allow students to edit text on cover and page 2.*
- *Save Publisher cards as pdf and email to family/friends.*

- *Take cards to a rest home to share with those who won't get many cards.*
- *Instead of a holiday card, create a community service card.*
- *Instead of holiday card, create a flier—very simple (see inset).*
- *Offer websites on start page that tie into class conversation.*
- *If this lesson doesn't work for your student group, use one from **How to Jumpstart the Inquiry-based Classroom.** It has 5 additional projects aligned with the SL curriculum.*

More Information:
- *Technology is pervasive in education. For more information, read "The Elephantine Impact of Technology on Education" on next pages.*
- *Lesson questions? Go to http://askatechteacher.com*
- *Second grade teaching wiki: http://smaatechk-3.wikispaces.com/This+Week+in+Tech—Second+Grade*
- *PDF: See appendix for bonus websites*
- *Follow keyboard lessons in K-8 Keyboard Curriculum (http://ow.ly/j6GH8)*

If you don't get through everything, check completed items so you know what to get back to when you have time on later lessons. I find as I focus on the central idea of a lesson, clarifying questions sometimes take more time than I'd expect. I'm fine with that. There'll be lessons later that move faster than I planned.

- **What do you call a computer superhero?**

  A Screen Saver.

- **Why did the computer cross the road?**

  To get a byte to eat.

- **What do you get if you cross a computer with an elephant?**

  Lots of Memory.

- **What do you get when you cross a dog and a computer?**

  A machine that has a bark worse than its byte.

- **Why was the computer so angry?**

  Because it had a chip on its shoulder.

- **Why did the computer get glasses?**

The Elephantine Impact of Technology on Education

Have you noticed what's happening in your child's school? If you haven't been in the classroom lately, drop by this week when you pick up your wonderful student. There's likely to be a SmartScreen on the wall, a pod of computers or 1:1 laptops overflowing from a corner, iPads on desktops or in a mobile cart, a digital camera and microphones to record events, streaming video from Discovery  Channel—all examples of the digital tools that now scaffold education. Those ubiquitous samples of student work that traditionally clutter walls now include many created with computers. There's rarely a lesson taught, be it math or science or health, that doesn't include technologic tools to enhance the message, increase its reach, and improve its communication.

Today, education excels by standing on the shoulders of technology innovation.

As a tech teacher, the new educational paradigm relies on either the United States' No Child Left Behind, the International Baccalaureate Organization's educational guidelines, and/or the National Board of Governors state-driven Common Core Standards. Interestingly, these education standards address technology as they contribute to core subjects. Many states continue to have technology standards, but many others leave it to the International Society of Technology Education's well-respected national technology standards. Where I used to teach keyboarding and software. Now, it's laptops, iPads, online tools, websites, and problem-solving to increase independence.

What a wonderful time to be a student.

Lesson #14—Around the World I

Vocabulary	Problem solving	Big Idea
Continents *Digital tools* *Drill down* *Legend* *Network* *Poles* *Resize* *Rubric* *Template* *Text box*	*I can't find my project (save early save often)* *I lost my project (use Windows Search)* *How do I print (Ctrl+P)* *How do I save (Ctrl+S)* *Fill flowed out of section I wanted to color (connect edges)* *Label's in wrong spot (drag to right spot)*	*Sometimes, visual representation of data is clearer than text*
Time Required *45 minutes*	**NETS-S Standards** 4c, 6b	**CCSS** *CCSS.ELA-Literacy.W.2.6*

Essential Question
How can I use a picture to share information?

Overview

Materials

Internet, template, drawing program, keyboarding program

Teacher Preparation
- Talk with classroom teacher so you tie into conversations on planet, oceans, continents
- Have template on network so students can access
- Know what image format is required to display template, i.e., does drawing program require .bmp or .jpg or another image standard?
- Have rubrics available for early finishers
- Is class shorter than 45 minutes? Highlight items most important to your integration with core classroom studies and leave the rest for 'later'.

Steps

_____Warm up by keyboarding QWERTY or lower row with an online site like DanceMat Typing and Nimble Fingers (Google names for addresses):

- *Hands— home row position, curved over keys*
- *Posture—centered in front of keyboard, legs in front of body*

_____Discuss planet's continents, oceans. What are students discussing in class?

_____'Around the World' project takes two weeks. Open drawing program on SmartScreen and demonstrate (we use KidPix, but you can use TuxPaint, Paint, other). Import template to be used, like this Enchanted Learning globe.

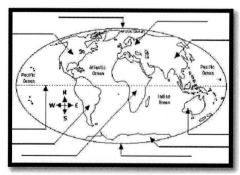

_____Before students start project, ask them to notice what digital tools they are using. Consider others that might accomplish same goals. Word? Publisher? Kerpoof? Which have students used? This is a good opportunity to transfer knowledge.

_____Add student name with text tool (size 36).

_____Add continent and ocean names (size 10). Show how to resize text boxes to fit provided lines. Watch grammar. Check spelling against sample on next pages.

_____When done, save to network folder. Make sure student last name is in file name. Why? (see completed sample on next page).

_____Throughout class, check for understanding. Expect students to solve problems and make decisions that follow class rules.

_____Remind students to transfer knowledge to classroom or home.

_____As you teach, incorporate lesson vocabulary. Check this line if you did that today!

_____Close with Alt+F4. Tuck chairs under desk, headphones over tower; leave station as it was.

Assessment Strategies
- *Followed directions*
- *Remembered skills from previous lessons*
- *Joined class conversation*
- *Understood digital tools being used*

Trouble-shooting:
- *Drawing program won't save? Take a screen shot (using Jing, Snippet, or similar).*
- *Time tight? Have students label only continents or oceans.*
- *Can't import template into drawing program? Is it right file type, i.e., jpg?*
- *You have print book and need website? Pick grade level and search (Alt+F) name on https://askatechteacher.wordpress.com/great-websites-for-kids.*

Extension:
- *As you teach, mention shortkeys as often as possible. For many students, they are easier to use. Once comfortable with these key combinations, tech will be more fun.*
- *Do project as a group—you on SmartScreen, students at their computers.*
- *Offer additional websites on subjects that tie into class conversation.*
- *If this lesson doesn't work for your students, use one from **How to Jumpstart the Inquiry-based Classroom.** It has 5 projects aligned with the SL curriculum.*

More Information:
- *Lesson questions? Go to http://askatechteacher.com*
- *Second grade teaching wiki: http://smaatechk-3.wikispaces.com/This+Week+in+Tech—Second+Grade*
- *PDF: See appendix for bonus websites*
- *Follow keyboard lessons in K-8 Keyboard Curriculum (http://ow.ly/j6GH8)*

If you don't get through everything, check completed items so you know what to get back to when you have time on later lessons. I find as I focus on the central idea of a lesson, clarifying questions sometimes take more time than I'd expect. I'm fine with that. There'll be lessons later that move faster than I planned.

'Around the World' Samples
Top: template with directions
Bottom: completed example

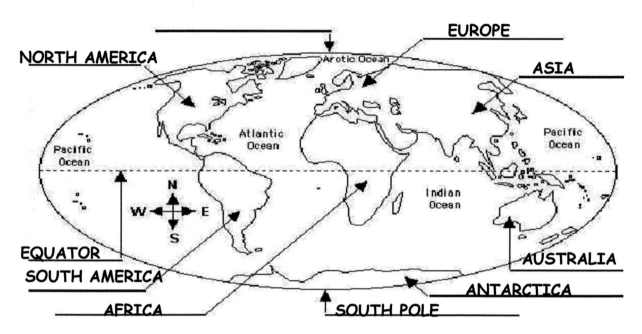

Template credit: Enchanted Learning

1. Color Africa green
2. Color Antarctica white
3. Color Asia yellow
4. Color Australia brown

5. Color Europe red
6. Color No. America orange
7. Color So. America pink
8. Color oceans blue

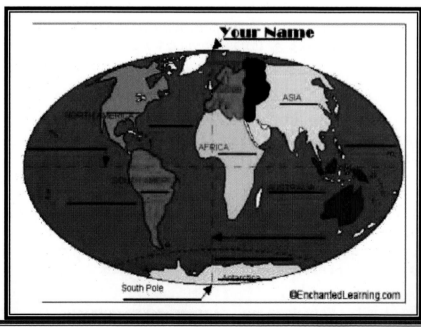

Lesson #15— Around the World II

Vocabulary	Problem solving	Big Idea
🔲 Continents 🔲 Drill down 🔲 Fill 🔲 Legend 🔲 Network 🔲 Paint bucket 🔲 Poles 🔲 Resize 🔲 Rubric 🔲 Template 🔲 Text box 🔲 Text tool	🔲 My monitor doesn't work (wake up mouse, check power) 🔲 My computer doesn't work (check power, check plug) 🔲 What's the difference between 'export' and 'save' (in KidPix, 'export' saves project in a format that can be viewed in other programs) 🔲 How do I print? 🔲 Why can't I save to 'My Documents' (It's not part of network) 🔲 I can't find my project (try 'search')	*Sometimes, visual representation of data is clearer than text*
Time Required *45 minutes*	**NETS-S Standards** *4c, 6b*	**CCSS** *CCSS.ELA-Literacy.W.2.6*

Essential Question
How can I use a picture to share information?

Overview

Materials

Internet, project template and rubric, keyboarding program

Teacher Preparation

- Talk with class teacher so you tie into their inquiry on planet, oceans, continents
- Have rubrics available
- Have websites on class internet start page for those who finish
- Is class shorter than 45 minutes? Highlight items most important to your integration with core classroom studies and leave the rest for 'later'

Steps

_____This is week two of Around the World. Today, students color continents labeled last week. Use a legend (what's a legend? What have students discussed in class about 'legends'?).

_____Open KidPix. Open project started last week. If students have trouble finding, check 'My Documents'; if not there, use 'search'.

_____Use paint bucket tool to color as directed on legend at end of this

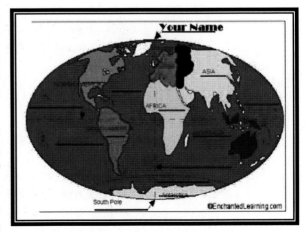

lesson. If color flows into ocean or wrong continent, undo and fill in black line that separates sections

_____Check rubric checklist for assessment details (see following pages). Students complete and submit today.

_____Export (rather than save) so this picture can be used in Open House slideshow. Print with Ctrl+P.

_____As students finish, poll them on two topics:

- *What digital tool did they use to create this project?*
- *What other digital tools might have been used instead? It can be one they've used in class or at home*

_____Those who finish: Practice lower row keyboarding on online program. Remember: Hands curved over home row, good posture; legs in front of body, keyboard in front of body, mouse to the right.

_____As you teach, incorporate lesson vocabulary. Check this line if you did that today!

Assessment Strategies
- *Anecdotal observation*
- *Finished project*
- *Finished rubric*
- *Followed directions*

_____Continually throughout class, check for understanding. Expect students to solve problems as they maneuver through lesson and make decisions that follow class rules.

_____Remind students to transfer this knowledge to the classroom or home.

_____Tuck chairs under desk, headphones over tower; leave station as you found it.

Trouble-shooting:
- *If fill flows into multiple parts of template, show why this happens (edges aren't snugged) and how to fix (use pencil tool to connect edges).*
- *Student forgot to print? Show them how to access their network folder from 'Computer', then right click and print.*
- *Can't print from file folder? Did student save in KidPix rather than export? If so, open file in KidPix and export. Then, it will print.*
- *You have print book and need website? Pick grade level and search name (Ctrl+F) at https://askatechteacher.wordpress.com/great-websites-for-kids/.*

Extension:
- *Use KidPix sticker tool to add country flags. Make student country of origin largest.*
- *Add a compass rose to map; discuss what this is; tie into class discussion.*
- *Make poll student-directed. As students finish their project, invite them up to the SmartScreen. Have a PollDaddy poll suggesting which digital tools were used that day. Have students check off all used. Click inset to vote!*

- *Offer additional websites on subjects that tie into class conversation.*
- *If this lesson doesn't work for your students, use one from **How to Jumpstart the Inquiry-based Classroom.** It has 5 projects aligned with SL curriculum.*

More Information:
- *Lesson questions? Go to http://askatechteacher.com*
- *Second grade teaching wiki:*
  http://smaatechk-3.wikispaces.com/This+Week+in+Tech—Second+Grade
- *PDF: See appendix for bonus websites*
- *Follow keyboard lessons in K-8 Keyboard Curriculum (http://ow.ly/j6GH8)*

If you don't get through everything, check completed items so you know what to get back to when you have time on later lessons. I find as I focus on the central idea of a lesson, clarifying questions sometimes take more time than I'd expect. I'm fine with that. There'll be lessons later that move faster than I planned.

Around the World
Grading Rubric

Your name: _____

Teacher: _____

1. Map colored as required	__5 points__
a. Oceans blue	_____
b. Continents per legend	_____
2. Continents labeled	__5 points__
a. In correct spot	_____
b. Readable	_____
c. Fonts/sizes correct	_____
3. Your name on project	__5 points__

Lesson #16—About Me: A Summative Project

Vocabulary	Problem solving	Big Idea
🖳 *Backspace* 🖳 *Conventions* 🖳 *Delete* 🖳 *Edit* 🖳 *Export* 🖳 *Font* 🖳 *Grammar* 🖳 *Punctuation* 🖳 *Shift key* 🖳 *Slideshow* 🖳 *Text tool*	🖳 *How do I close program (Alt+F4)* 🖳 *Program disappeared (check taskbar)* 🖳 *My typing disappeared (Ctrl+Z)* 🖳 *When do I use backspace and when do I use delete?* 🖳 *My text covers picture (drag text box to a different location)* 🖳 *What's the difference between export and save?*	*It is easier to communicate ideas when using good language conventions*
Time Required *45 minutes*	**NETS-S Standards** *2b, 6b*	**CCSS** *CCSS.ELA-Literacy.L.2.1*

Essential Question
Can I use my knowledge of language conventions to tell my story?

Overview

Materials

Internet, drawing program, keyboarding program

Teacher Preparation

- Talk with classroom teacher so you tie into their teaching on grammar and spelling
- Discuss story construction (Brilliant Beginning, Mighty Middle, Exciting Ending)
- Is class shorter than 45 minutes? Highlight items most important to your integration with core classroom studies and leave the rest for 'later'.

Steps

_____Today's project starts a slideshow story students will prepare for Open House, following class writing guidelines. It includes details to describe actions, thoughts, and feelings, temporal words to signal event order, and a sense of closure. It celebrates tech skills accomplished during second grade (tools, toolbars, fills, drag-and-drop, backgrounds, clipart, and more).

_____Allow one week to practice, one to save, if necessary.

_____Open drawing software (KidPix, Paint, TuxPaint, Kerpoof, other. Here, we use KidPix).

_____Explain project to students. They start with a picture to introduce themselves with two well-structured, grammatically-correct sentences, using grammar, spelling and story writing conventions discussed in class (i.e., your school's version of Brilliant Beginning, Mighty Middle, Exciting Ending).

_____Demonstrate on SmartScreen: Draw a picture using five colors. Use thick pencil.

_____Use text tool to write two sentences in font 48 (pick font and color; make it '**Bold**') to introduce story, i.e., "Once upon a time, there was a girl/boy named ***. S/he *** (tell me something about her/him). BUT: Add no punctuation. What do students think? Do they understand the meaning? Discuss.

_____Ask students how to edit to be clearer. Have them come up and show where punctuation and grammar goes.

_____Ask how to edit—with backspace or delete?

_____Encourage students to complete this project as independently as possible. They've used the tools before. Remind them rather than teach. Leave sample on SmartScreen.

_____Remind students: Every time they use the computer, practice good keyboard skills.

_____Export picture with minimal assistance. Why export rather than save?

_____Those who finish: Practice keyboarding lower row using an online program like DanceMat Typing or Nimble Fingers.

_____As you teach, incorporate lesson vocabulary. Check this line if you did that today!

_____Continually throughout class, check for understanding. Expect students to solve problems as they maneuver through lesson and make decisions that follow class rules.

_____Remind students to transfer knowledge to classroom and home.

_____Tuck chairs under desk, headphones over tower; leave station as you found it.

Assessment Strategies
- Completed project
- Exported successfully
- Transferred skills from prior project
- Demonstrated command of writing conventions (per Common Core

Trouble-shooting:
- *Drawing program won't allow saving? Take a screen shot and save that (using Jing, Snippet, or similar).*
- *You have print book and need website? Pick grade level and search (Ctrl+F) name on https://askatechteacher.wordpress.com/great-websites-for-kids/.*

Extension:
- *This can be a summative or formative assessment as it uses skills already learned.*
- *Use KidPix Animations (dog tool)—'alphabet' for student name.*
- *Those who finish early: Practice spelling/site words on SpellingCity.com.*
- *Offer additional websites on subjects that tie into class inquiry.*
- *Anytime you can inject tech into the class, do it! Students love seeing gadgets in action. For example—take a video of students working at their computers and upload to class website/blog/wiki.*

- *If this lesson doesn't work for your student group, use one from **How to Jumpstart the Inquiry-based Classroom.** It has 5 additional projects aligned with SL curriculum.*

More Information:
- *Lesson questions? Go to http://askatechteacher.com*
- *Second grade teaching wiki:*
  http://smaatechk-3.wikispaces.com/This+Week+in+Tech—Second+Grade
- *PDF: See appendix for bonus websites*
- *Follow keyboard lessons in K-8 Keyboard Curriculum (http://ow.ly/j6GH8)*

If you don't get through everything, check completed items so you know what to get back to when you have time on later lessons. I find as I focus on the central idea of a lesson, clarifying questions sometimes take more time than I'd expect. I'm fine with that. There'll be lessons later that move faster than I planned.

Helpdesk:	**Double click "My Computer"**
User:	**I can't see your computer.**
Helpdesk:	**No, double click "My Computer" on your computer.**
User:	**Huh?**
Helpdesk:	**There is an icon on your computer labeled "My Computer". Double click it.**
User:	**What's your computer doing on mine?**

Lesson #17—Develop Details

Vocabulary	Problem solving	Big Idea
Characters *Color (detail)* *Conventions* *Digital tool* *Edit* *Grammar* *Network* *Palette* *Plot* *Sentence fluency* *Setting* *Voice*	*How do I capitalize (use shift key)* *Capital stuck (check caps lock)* *What's my user name? (check with teacher)* *What's the difference between backspace and delete?* *What's the difference between edit and format?* *Do I save or export? (it depends upon what the purpose is)* *Do I save or 'save-as'?* *Where's the network?*	***Recount a story with words and pictures including a sense of closure***
Time Required *45 minutes*	**NETS-S Standards** *2b, 4b*	**CCSS** *CCSS.ELA-Literacy.W.2.3*

Essential Question
How does detail enhance the power of a story?

Overview

Materials

Internet, SmartScreen, word processing program, story from a first grader

Teacher Preparation
- Talk with classroom teacher so you tie into their teaching on grammar and spelling
- Discuss basics of story construction (Brilliant Beginning, Mighty Middle, Exciting Ending) with classroom teacher
- List websites on internet start page that support classroom inquiry
- Is class shorter than 45 minutes? Highlight items most important to your integration with core classroom studies and leave the rest for 'later'

Steps

_____Circle back on word processing skills in this lesson and review how to edit.

_____Show students a story that a first grader wrote. What makes this story sound immature? For example:

- *Insufficient detail about characters*
- *Insufficient detail about setting*
- *Words are too simple.*
- *Words are repetitive*

_____Student writing skills have grown tremendously since first grade. They now know how to provide detail, color, a sense of time, and how to make a story more interesting.

_____Show this story on class SmartScreen (without yellow bubbles):

> *Coyote was very old. His fur was mangy and falling out in spots. And his bright white teeth had yellowed with the diet of grasses he ate. He had...*

"Mr. Coyote was getting very <u>old</u> and had to be more careful for his own safety. He had been <u>walking</u> for hours and hours through a <u>beautiful</u> valley when he came upon a large tree. Mr. Coyote was very tired and wanted to <u>rest</u> but he also needed to be safe. He kindly asked the tree, "Please open up so I can rest safely in your care".

> *Its trunk was craggy and thick, and its arms spread wide over the grass as though welcoming Mr. Coyote.*

_____Read it to students. Are they drawn in? Why or why not? What else would they like to know?

_____Now read yellow bubbles with changes you (or they) suggest. Use these to start a conversation on how to enhance the story. For example:

- *Sentence fluency*
- *Word choice*
- *Voice*
- *Writing conventions*
- *Organization*
- *Idea development*

_____As students make suggestions, write them on SmartScreen and add as many as possible to story.

_____When done, ask if students are more intrigued by the story?

_____Have students open a word processing program with a partner (Word, Google Docs, Open Office, KidPix). Add a heading with both partner names. Copy this short story from the SmartScreen:

I play basketball. I love to play basketball.. I like to play against my brother. He told me when you stop dribbling, you can't start dribbling again.

_____Discuss as a class how this story might be 'fixed' so it is more exciting:

- *Why does s/he love to play basketball?*
- *Why does s/he like to play against her/his brother?*
- *What was the importance of 'dribbling'?*
- *What does it feel like to play basketball?*

- *How can you add variety to the words 'play', 'dribbling', 'basketball'?*

_____Have students type the story and edit with partner (should they use backspace or delete?). If necessary, review class guidelines for speaking and listening:

- *Gain the floor in respectful ways*
- *Listen to others with care*
- *Speak one at a time about topics and texts under discussion*
- *Build on others' talk by linking to their remarks*
- *Ask for clarification and further explanation as needed*

Assessment Strategies

- *Observed student speaking and listening skills (per Common Core guidelines)*
- *Transferred knowledge of writing conventions*
- *Worked well with a partner*
- *Joined class discussions*

_____When done, have groups share changes they made with class. Is anyone surprised by how different everyone's changes are?

_____As you teach, incorporate lesson vocabulary. Check this line if you did that today!

_____Save in student network folder.

Trouble-shooting:
- *When students have a problem that you determine has been covered in prior lessons, ask class for help. But, don't point out who didn't know the answer.*
- *Sometimes you need more than one week for a lesson. No worries. There are 32 lessons in text, 35ish in school year. Feel free to stretch a lesson a week or more.*
- *You have print book and need website? Pick grade level and search (Ctrl+F) name on https://askatechteacher.wordpress.com/great-websites-for-kids/.*

Extension:
- *Practice site words in SpellingCity.com.*
- *Offer additional websites on subjects that tie into class conversation.*

More Information:
- *Lesson questions? Go to http://askatechteacher.com*
- *Second grade teaching wiki:*
  http://smaatechk-3.wikispaces.com/This+Week+in+Tech—Second+Grade
- *PDF: See appendix for bonus websites*
- *Follow keyboard lessons in K-8 Keyboard Curriculum (http://ow.ly/j6GH8)*

If you don't get through everything, check completed items so you know what to get back to when you have time on later lessons. I find as I focus on the central idea of a lesson, clarifying questions sometimes take more time than I'd expect. I'm fine with that. There'll be lessons later that move faster than I planned.

Lesson #18—Where I Live

Vocabulary	Problem solving	Big Idea
▣ *Alt* ▣ *Detail* ▣ *Edit* ▣ *Export* ▣ *Format* ▣ *Grammar* ▣ *Icon* ▣ *Palette* ▣ *Setting*	▣ *How do I capitalize (shift key)* ▣ *Cap won't go off (check caps lock)* ▣ *What's a user name? (ask teacher)* ▣ *What's the date (Shift+Alt+D)* ▣ *What's the difference between 'save' and 'export'?* ▣ *What's the difference between backspace and delete?* ▣ *How do I exit? (Alt+F4)*	*Recount a story with words and pictures including a sense of closure*
Time Required *45 minutes*	**NETS-S Standards** *2b, 4b*	**CCSS** *CCSS.ELA-Literacy.W.2.3*

Essential Question
How does detail enhance the power of a story?

Overview

Materials

    Internet, drawing program, SmartScreen, keyboarding program

Teacher Preparation

- Talk with classroom teacher so you tie into their teaching on the basics of story construction (i.e., Brilliant Beginning, Mighty Middle, Exciting Ending)
- Is your class shorter than 45 minutes? Highlight items most important to your integration with core classroom studies and leave the rest for 'later'.

Steps

_____Today's project continues a four-drawing series that students are preparing for Open House. These slides recount a story, including details to describe actions, thoughts, and feelings, temporal words to signal event order, and a sense of closure. It also celebrates tech skills accomplished during second grade (tools, toolbars, fills, drag-and-drop, backgrounds, clipart and more.

_____Be prepared to allow students one week to practice, one to save, if necessary.

_____Open drawing software (i.e., KidPix, Paint, TuxPaint, Kerpoof, or other. We use KidPix in this example).

_____Last week, students created the Brilliant Beginning. Today, it's time for the Mighty Middle: Provide detail to your story with two well-structured, grammatically-correct sentences.

_____Demonstrate on SmartScreen as you illustrate story setting.

_____Write first sentence. Does it tell students enough? What else would they like to know? Think back to last lesson.

_____Add detail suggested by students as second sentence. How should it be punctuated?

_____Now students open drawing program. Use paint brush tool to draw house with building materials and landscaping items. Feel free to change color of trees, grass, etc. with color palette. Don't cover entire screen with brick—we should see 'white' on three sides.

_____Write a sentence in font 48, then add a sentence that provides detail on setting. Try different fonts. Select color with palette.

_____Work with neighbor to:

- *elaborate on event or add a short sequence of events*
- *add detail to describe actions, thoughts, feelings*
- *add temporal words to signal event order*

_____Export to student network folder. Use Alt+F4 to exit.

_____Remind students: Every time they use the computer, practice good keyboarding skills.

_____Done? Practice typing lower row on online keyboarding program. Type with correct posture and hand position, elbows at side, no flying fingers or flying hands.

_____As you teach, incorporate lesson vocabulary. Check this line if you did that today!

_____Continually throughout class, check for understanding. Expect students to solve problems as they maneuver through lesson and make decisions that follow class rules.

_____Remind students to transfer knowledge to classroom or home.

_____Tuck chairs under desk, headphones over tower; leave station as you found it.

Assessment Strategies

- *Anecdotal observation*
- *Completed project*
- *Transferred writing skills from classroom to project*
- *Worked well with partner; followed general rules for collaboration*

Trouble-shooting:

- *Drawing program won't allow saving? Take a screen shot and save that (using Jing, Snippet, or similar).*
- *When students have a problem covered in prior lessons, ask the class for help. But, don't point out who didn't know the answer.*

- Occasionally when students have difficulty doing what you are teaching, ask why. And listen. You may be surprised by the answer.
- Sometimes you need more than one week for a lesson. No worries. There are 32 lessons in text, 35ish in school year. Feel free to stretch a lesson a week or more.
- You have print book and need website? Pick grade level and search (Ctrl+F) name on https://askatechteacher.wordpress.com/great-websites-for-kids/.

Extension:
- Offer additional websites on subjects that tie into class conversation.
- Replace lesson with 1st Grade lesson #2 Brainstorm Ideas in curriculum extendors (http://www.structuredlearning.net/book/k-6-curriculum-extender/).

More Information:
- Lesson questions? Go to http://askatechteacher.com
- Second grade teaching wiki: http://smaatechk-3.wikispaces.com/This+Week+in+Tech—Second+Grade
- PDF: See appendix for bonus websites
- Follow keyboard lessons in K-8 Keyboard Curriculum (http://ow.ly/j6GH8)

If you don't get through everything, check completed items so you know what to get back to when you have time on later lessons. I find as I focus on the central idea of a lesson, clarifying questions sometimes take more time than I'd expect. I'm fine with that. There'll be lessons later that move faster than I planned.

> **"Do you have a sledge-hammer?"**
>
> *— Top comment you don't want to hear from Tech Support*

Lesson #19—Valentine Greeting

Vocabulary	Problem solving	Big Idea
▨ Border ▨ Export ▨ Font ▨ Format ▨ Grammar ▨ Greeting ▨ Handles ▨ Heading ▨ Image ▨ Tools ▨ Word processing ▨ Wrap	▨ I can't exit (Alt+F4) ▨ I can't print (file-print or Ctrl+P) ▨ How do I get text on next line (let it wrap by itself) ▨ How do I know letter fits one page (check the bar at bottom of page— does it say '1 of 1'?) ▨ How do I resize an image (handles) ▨ How do I fix spelling (right click on word and select correct spelling) ▨ Why do I have to learn Word (or other word processing program)?	*It's important to pick the right technology for the intended purpose*
Time Required *45 minutes*	**NETS-S Standards** *4b, 6b*	**CCSS** *CCSS.ELA-Literacy*

Essential Question

Why is Word (or another word processing program) the best choice for a letter or report?

Overview

Materials

Internet, word processing program, printer, keyboard website, kid-safe image websites

Teacher Preparation

- Talk with classroom teacher to understand what students know about letter writing, grammar at this point in year
- Have websites on class start page that tie into classroom conversation
- Is class shorter than 45 minutes? Highlight items most important to your integration with core classroom studies and leave the rest for 'later'.

Steps

_____Today, students will create a Valentine letter in Word (or other word processing program used in your school like Google Docs, Open Office. We use Word for this example). This is ongoing preparation for the summative report students will complete at the end of school year requiring a word processing competency. By circling back on basic skills several times, students gain confidence in their ability.

_____Ask students: Why Word? Why not Publisher (or another desktop publisher)? Why not PowerPoint or Excel? Discuss how to select the right program for particular needs.

_____Students know Word basics. This is an authentic assessment of their progress.

_____Open MS Word. Write a letter that includes greeting, body—3 to 5 sentences, close. Use font size 48, any font look and color. Make sure student name is in closing or at top. As active learners, students should think back to how they added borders, images, changed fonts.

_____When typing is done, add two-three images that communicate same message as words. Use clipart if in Word, Google images if not. If going online for images, remind students how to use the internet safely.

_____Done? Work with neighbor to check:

- *Are grammar and spelling good—red and green squiggles? What's blue line?*
- *Does letter fit one page? If not, resize images.*
- *Is everything included? If not, edit.*

_____When corrected, print without help. Save (or save as?) without help; back-up to flash drive if appropriate.

_____As you teach, incorporate lesson vocabulary. Check this line if you did that today!

_____Continually throughout class, check for understanding. Expect students to solve problems as they maneuver through lesson and make decisions that follow class rules.

_____Remind students: Every time they use the computer, practice good keyboarding skills

_____This is a one-week project, so students print whatever they get done. The results will help you assess learning.

_____Those who finish: Practice keyboarding lower row on online program.

_____Close to desktop with Alt+F4. Leave station clean and neat, chair tucked under, headphones over tower, text behind monitor.

_____Remind students to transfer knowledge to classroom or home.

> **Your name**
>
> Dear Mom and Dad
>
> **HAPPY VALENTINE DAY!**
> **I love you.**
> You are the best.
>
> *Love,*
> *Your name*

Assessment Strategies
- *Anecdotal observation*
- *Completed project*
- *Used proper grammar and spelling*
- *Worked well with partner*

Trouble-shooting:
- *Hardware problems? Have students try to solve them before asking for assistance.*
- *Sometimes you need more than one week for a lesson. No worries. There are 32 lessons in text, 35ish in school year. Feel free to stretch a lesson a week or more.*
- *You have print book and need website? Pick grade level and search (Ctrl+F) name on https://askatechteacher.wordpress.com/great-websites-for-kids/.*

Extension:
- *Have students look at Lesson 9 samples and pick one a step harder than what they completed back then.*

- *Have students create this project in a desktop publishing program like Publisher. Which did they like better? What were the differences?*
- *Offer websites on subjects that tie into class inquiry.*
- *If this lesson doesn't work for your student group, use one from **How to Jumpstart the Inquiry-based Classroom.** It has 5 projects aligned with the SL curriculum.*

More Information:
- *Lesson questions? Go to http://askatechteacher.com*
- *Second grade teaching wiki: http://smaatechk-3.wikispaces.com/This+Week+in+Tech—Second+Grade*
- *PDF: See appendix for bonus websites*
- *Follow keyboard lessons in K-8 Keyboard Curriculum (http://ow.ly/j6GH8)*

If you don't get through everything, check completed items so you know what to get back to when you have time on later lessons. I find as I focus on the central idea of a lesson, clarifying questions sometimes take more time than I'd expect. I'm fine with that. There'll be lessons later that move faster than I planned.

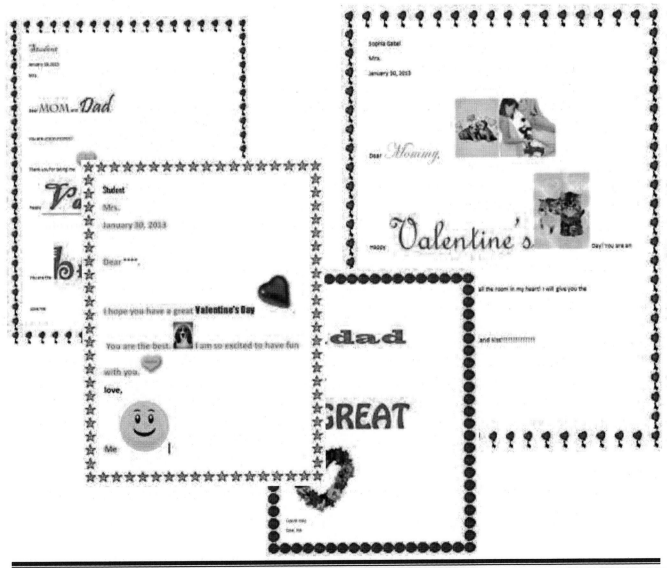

Lesson #20—Stories With Words/Pictures

Vocabulary	Problem solving	Big Idea
▪ *Closure* ▪ *Cursor* ▪ *Edit* ▪ *Export* ▪ *Flash drive* ▪ *Font* ▪ *Format* ▪ *Lower row* ▪ *Network* ▪ *Plot* ▪ *Temporal* ▪ *Tool bar*	▪ *Can't find file folder (check log-in. Are you in correct profile?)* ▪ *Can't find project (did you export or save?)* ▪ *How do I save to flash drive?* ▪ *What's the difference between save and save-as?* ▪ *How do I save to network?* ▪ *How do I edit? (backspace/delete)* ▪ *How do I move cursor?* ▪ *Why is my last name in file name?* ▪ *Text covers picture (move text)*	***Recount a story with words and pictures including a sense of closure***
Time Required *45 minutes*	**NETS-S Standards** *2b, 4b*	**CCSS** *CCSS.ELA-Literacy.W.2.3*

Essential Question
Can I use pictures to share details like temporal order and closure?

Overview
Materials

Internet, drawing program, keyboard program

Teacher Preparation
- Talk with classroom teacher so you tie into their conversations on writing
- If there's word study, get the list (if doing Extension)
- Is class shorter than 45 minutes? Highlight items most important to integration with core classroom studies and leave the rest for 'later'.

Steps

_____This is the third of four Open House slides that recount a story, including details to describe actions, thoughts, and feelings, temporal words to signal event order, and a sense of closure. This picture is the 'plot'. Discuss meaning of terms like 'temporal' and 'signal event order'.

_____Open drawing program (KidPix, TuxPaint, or other program used at your school. We will use KidPix).

_____Add sentence, size 48, your choice of font and color. This is the action, the drama, a problem main character solves or a wish s/he has.

_____Use correct grammar and spelling.

Right now, I'm (playing soccer and the violin), but when I grow up, I want to be (a heart surgeon)

Capitalize first letter, space between words, and period at end of sentence. Remind students to use backspace and delete to edit from where cursor blinks.

_____Use five different brushes, five colors, to draw picture. Check that title doesn't cover picture. If it does, move text box or resize text.

_____Before exporting: Check that picture and text deliver same message. If not, edit.

_____Export to network folder.

_____Finished? Practice keyboarding lower row on typing website. Remember correct posture and hand position.

_____As you teach, incorporate lesson vocabulary. Check this line if you did that today!

_____Continually throughout class, check for understanding. Expect students to solve problems as they maneuver through lesson and make decisions that follow class rules.

_____Remind students to transfer knowledge to classroom or home.

_____Tuck chairs under desk, headphones over tower; leave station as you found it.

One day she wished for...
A horse.

Assessment Strategies
- *Completed project*
- *Transferred knowledge from class to lab*
- *Self-corrected*

Trouble-shooting:
- *Drawing program won't allow saving? Take a screen shot and save that (using Jing, Snippet, or similar).*
- *Hardware problems? Let students try to solve before helping.*
- *Sometimes you need more than one week for a lesson. No worries. There are 32 lessons in text, 35ish in school year. Feel free to stretch a lesson a week or more.*
- *You have print book and need website? Pick grade level and search (Ctrl+F) name on https://askatechteacher.wordpress.com/great-websites-for-kids/.*

Extension:
- *This can be considered a formative assessment as it uses skills already learned.*
- *Do this project in Word also. Discuss differences with students. Which approach did they like better? You could also do it using an audio program like Voki. In this way, you can differentiate instruction for students who aren't 'writers'.*
- *Done? Use SpellingCity.com to review word study.*
- *If this lesson doesn't work for your student group, use one from **How to Jumpstart the Inquiry-based Classroom.** It has 5 additional projects aligned with the SL curriculum.*

More Information:

- *Lesson questions? Go to http://askatechteacher.com*
- *Second grade teaching wiki:*
  http://smaatechk-3.wikispaces.com/This+Week+in+Tech—Second+Grade
- *PDF: See appendix for bonus websites*
- *Follow keyboard lessons in K-8 Keyboard Curriculum (http://ow.ly/j6GH8)*

If you don't get through everything, check completed items so you know what to get back to when you have time on later lessons. I find as I focus on the central idea of a lesson, clarifying questions sometimes take more time than I'd expect. I'm fine with that. There'll be lessons later that move faster than I planned.

Login: yes
Password: I don't have one
password is incorrect

Login: yes
Password: incorrect
password is incorrect

Lesson #21—My Body

Vocabulary	Problem solving	Big Idea
Align *Alt+F4* *Default* *Dialogue box* *Export* *Handles* *Network* *Resize* *Server* *Template* *Text box*	*Program disappeared (check taskbar)* *Text box is too big (use handles to resize)* *Text is too big (reduce font size)* *I can't find template (try server)* *I can't find server (follow directions)* *My text boxes overlap (resize)* *I printed but it didn't work (did you print to the right printer?)*	*Typing information into a form helps me to remember what I'm studying*
Time Required *45 minutes*	**NETS-S Standards** *4a, 6a*	**CCSS** *CCSS.ELA-Literacy.SL.2.2*

Essential Question
How can a computer form I fill out help me remember information?

Overview

Materials

Internet, human body template, keyboarding program, human body websites

Teacher Preparation

- Talk with classroom teacher so you use the same human body terminology as they do (for example: Do they expect students to call the jawbone a 'mandible'?)
- Have human body template on server where students can access it
- Have list of human body websites on class internet start page
- Decide whether this is practice or a formative assessment
- Is class shorter than 45 minutes? Highlight items most important to integration with core classroom studies and leave rest for 'later'.

Steps

_____Introduce human body unit with this BrainPop video and answer questions at end as a group (http://www.brainpop.com/science/diversityoflife/humanbody/).

_____Providing a fill-in-the-blanks worksheet helps students remember information: 1) they type it, 2) they read what they type.

_____Demonstrate how to complete worksheet:

- *Open drawing program (we use KidPix).*
- *Show students how to find template on server and bring it into program (i.e., on EnchantedLearning.com).*

- *Fill in blanks with student collaboration on SmartScreen. Use body parts words from classroom. If they say 'jaw' in class, don't put 'mandible', and vice versa. This will be terms learned orally, in class text, from the video just watched, or other human body resources accessed as they studied this unit. Let them know you expect them to come up with as many parts as possible on their own. Vary this depending upon whether it is a formative or summative project.*
- *Use default font. Show students how to resize and move text box to align correctly on worksheet.*
- *Add skin color, then decorate with paint bucket, paint brush tool and stamps (skills students are familiar with).*

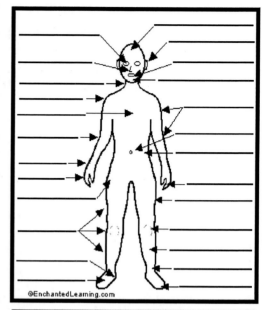

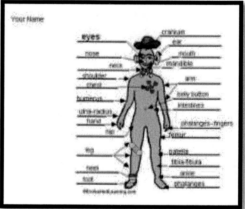

_____Now students complete theirs. Display sample (see end of lesson) on SmartScreen or use project as assessment.

_____Use paint bucket to color skin, paint brush to draw clothes, stamps to decorate.

_____Export without assistance; back-up to flash drive if available. Print.

_____Done? Practice keyboarding on installed software or online website. By now, students use entire keyboard rather than a row at a time.

_____As you teach, incorporate lesson vocabulary. Check this line if you did that!

_____Continually throughout class, check for understanding. Expect students to solve problems and make decisions.

_____Remind students to transfer knowledge to classroom or home.

_____Close to desktop; exit with Alt+F4 (why?).

_____Tuck chairs under desk, headphones over tower; leave station as you found it.

Assessment Strategies
- *Completed project*
- *Followed directions*
- *Transferred knowledge learned from other lessons*
- *Developing keyboard skills*

Trouble-shooting:

- *Print didn't work? Show students how to use correct printer.*
- *Drawing program won't save? Take screen shot (using Jing, Snippet, similar).*
- *Hardware problems? Have students try to solve before providing assistance.*
- *You have print book and need website? Pick grade level and search (Ctrl+F) name on https://askatechteacher.wordpress.com/great-websites-for-kids/.*
- *Sometimes you need more than a week per lesson. No worries. There are 32 in text, 35ish in school year. Feel free to stretch a lesson a week or more.*

Extension:
- *If this is NOT a formative/summative assessment, students can work in pairs.*
- *Done? Visit Human Body websites at end of this lesson.*
- *If this lesson doesn't work for your students, use one from **How to Jumpstart the Inquiry-based Classroom.** It has 5 projects aligned with SL curriculum.*

More Information:
- *Lesson questions? Go to http://askatechteacher.com*
- *Second grade teaching wiki: http://smaatechk-3.wikispaces.com/This+Week+in+Tech—Second+Grade*
- *PDF: See appendix for bonus websites*
- *Follow keyboard lessons in K-8 Keyboard Curriculum (http://ow.ly/j6GH8)*

If you don't get through everything, check completed items so you know what to get back to when you have time later. I find as I focus on the central idea of a lesson, clarifying questions sometimes take more time than I'd expect. I'm fine with that. There'll be lessons later that move faster than I planned.

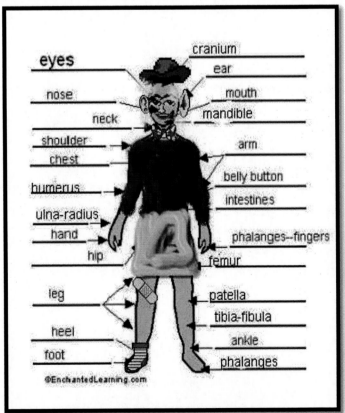

Human Body Websites

(No pdf? Go to http://askatechteacher.wordpress.com/great-websites-for-kids/human-body/)

- Blood Flow
- Body Systems
- Brain Pop—Body
- Build a Skeleton
- Build a Skeleton II
- Can you place these parts in the correct place?
- Choose the systems you want to see.
- Find My Body Parts
- Google Human Body
- Health games
- Health Games—BrainPop
- Heart Trek—Be the beat
- How the body works—videos
- Human body—interactive
- Human Body Games
- Human Body websites
- Human Body Websites II
- Human Body—by a 2nd grade class—video
- Human Body—videos on how body parts work
- Inside the Human Body: Grades 1-3
- Keep Ben Healthy
- Kid's Bio—Human Body
- Kids' Health-My Body
- Label the body
- Matching Senses
- Mr. Bones—put his body together
- Muscles Game
- Nutrition Music and Games from Dole
- Senses Challenge
- Weird stuff your body does

Lesson #22—The End (of the Slideshow)

Vocabulary	Problem solving	Big Idea
<ul><li>*Backspace*</li><li>*Closure*</li><li>*Cursor*</li><li>*Font*</li><li>*Multimedia*</li><li>*Network*</li><li>*PowerPoint*</li><li>*Publish*</li><li>*Slideshow*</li></ul>	<ul><li>*My volume doesn't work (check volume control)*</li><li>*My text covers picture (drag and move text box)*</li><li>*I made a mistake (edit)*</li><li>*What's the difference between backspace and delete?*</li><li>*How do I edit where I want to? (with cursor)*</li></ul>	***Recount a story with words and pictures including a sense of closure***
Time Required *45 minutes*	**NETS-S Standards** *1a, 6a*	**CCSS** *CCSS.ELA-Literacy.W.2.3*

Essential Question
Can I use pictures to share details like temporal order and closure?

Overview

Materials

Internet, drawing program, keyboard program

Teacher Preparation
- Talk with classroom teacher so you tie into conversations on story writing.
- Find out what grammar is being emphasized in class.
- Is class shorter than 45 minutes? Highlight items most important to integration with core classroom studies and leave the rest for 'later'.

Steps

_____This is the fourth and last slide in our story. It resolves the problem, provides the happy ending—includes a sense of closure. What is 'closure'?

_____Prepare students for upcoming PowerPoint unit by reminding them of Open House. What is PowerPoint? Remember last year?

_____Explain that each student will create a slideshow (a digital tool) to publish their writing and share the interdisciplinary array of skills learned this year with parents.

she got her new wings and lived happily ever after with her new friends!

_____Open drawing program (KidPix, TuxPaint, or other drawing program used at your school). This project uses skills students are comfortable with. Guide, assist where needed, but expect students to work independently.

_____Use paint bucket for background.

_____Use five different brushes, five colors, for picture.

_____Add a sentence in font size 48, choice of font and color, to wrap up story.

_____Use correct grammar and spelling. Remind students to use backspace and delete to edit from where cursor blinks.

_____Project inset to SmartScreen and ask students what is wrong with grammar. How should they edit it?

_____Check that text doesn't cover picture. If it does, move box.

_____Check that picture and text deliver the same message.

_____Export to student network folder.

_____Finished? Practice keyboarding on software or online website. Remember correct posture, correct hand position, and other typing habits.

_____Be sure to leave station as you found it (chairs in, desktop clean, headphones over tower, textbook behind monitor).

_____As you teach, incorporate lesson vocab. Check this line if you did that!

_____Throughout class, check for understanding. Expect students to solve problems as they maneuver through the lesson and make decisions that follow class rules.

_____Remind students to transfer knowledge to classroom or home.

Assessment Strategies

- *Completed project*
- *Transferred knowledge from classroom to lab*
- *Self-corrected as needed*
- *Slides tie into others and closes series of events*

Trouble-shooting:

- *Drawing program won't allow saving? Take a screen shot and save.*
- *Students turn monitors off so they don't have to figure out how to close down programs? Have them leave monitors on at end of class.*
- *You have print book and need website? Pick grade level and search (Alt+F) name on https://askatechteacher.wordpress.com/great-websites-for-kids/.*

Extension:

- *This can be a summative or formative assessment.*
- *Have students check network folders to see if they have required drawings. If not, create missing ones. You can show a sample on a corner of class SmartScreen.*
- *Offer additional websites on subjects that tie into class conversation.*
- *Replace this lesson with 2nd Grade Lesson #1 QR Me in curriculum extendors (http://www.structuredlearning.net/book/k-6-curriculum-extender/).*

More Information:

- *Lesson questions? Go to http://askatechteacher.com*
- *Second grade teaching wiki: http://smaatechk-3.wikispaces.com/This+Week+in+Tech—Second+Grade*
- *PDF: See appendix for bonus websites*
- *Follow keyboard lessons in K-8 Keyboard Curriculum (http://ow.ly/j6GH8)*

If you don't get through everything, check completed items so you know what to get back to when you have time on later lessons. I find as I focus on the central idea of a lesson, clarifying questions sometimes take more time than I'd expect. I'm fine with that. There'll be lessons later that move faster than I planned.

Lesson #23—Pictures from the Internet

Vocabulary	Problem solving	Big Idea
▓ *'scholarly research'* ▓ *Address bar* ▓ *Fair use* ▓ *Images* ▓ *Internet* ▓ *Public Domain* ▓ *Right-click menu* ▓ *Search* ▓ *Search bar* ▓ *Toggle* ▓ *Watermark*	▓ *I can't find the right pictures (try Google Images)* ▓ *I can't find my saved images (where did you save them?)* ▓ *One picture won't let me save (is it protected?)* ▓ *One picture has words on it (it's copyrighted—pick a different one)* ▓ *My picture came out weird (did you grab the thumbnail?)*	*I can collect information from a variety of sources and media to support my research*
Time Required *45 minutes*	**NETS-S Standards** *3b, 5a*	**CCSS** *CCSS.ELA-Literacy.W.2.8*

Essential Question

What's the right way to collect images from the internet?

Overview

Materials

Internet, specific websites, safe image websites, network folders

Teacher Preparation

- Talk with classroom teacher so you tie into their conversations
- Have Digital Citizenship posters up in discussion
- Have kid-safe image websites listed on class internet start page if required. Or have Google set to 'safe mode' if this is your approach
- Confirm that student network folders are available
- Is class shorter than 45 minutes? Highlight items most important to integration with core classroom studies and leave the rest for 'later'.

Steps

_____Today starts the first of four weeks on a report students will write in class and publish during tech time. Students will be asked to gather information from online sources that answer questions posed in the classroom (in this sample, *Life Cycle of an animal*). Today, we will find web-based pictures to support inquiry.

_____Before starting, remind students of conversations in prior weeks about safe use of internet. See internet websites in 'Extensions' at end of lesson if necessary.

_____Review Netiquette poster at end of lesson. What are student thoughts? Some of the points will be more important in later years.

_____Students will draw on knowledge learned in the classroom about stages in their animal's life cycle, to know which internet images to use. For example, one butterfly stage is 'caterpillar'. Students should know this without prompting.

_____Type animal name in website search bar (for 'chicks', use 'chickens' or 'baby chickens' instead). Select 'Images' and search.

_____Find animal picture (i.e., *lady bug*). Explain how to determine if picture is freely-available or copy-righted. Discuss 'public domain'. Why are pictures posted on Google Images (or Bing) if not free? This is a subject students will cover in much detail by the end of fifth grade.

_____Review image and copyright posters at end of this lesson.

_____Wrap up discussion by letting students know they can use these pictures for 'scholarly research'. Then, their use falls under 'fair use' and that's fine for schoolwork.

_____Right click on picture; 'save image as' to network file. No need to change name.

_____Repeat until student has one picture for each life cycle stage.

_____As you teach, incorporate lesson vocabulary. Check this line if you did that today!

_____Continually throughout class, check for understanding. Expect students to solve problems and make decisions.

_____Remind students to transfer knowledge to classroom or home.

_____Close down to desktop; Tuck chairs under desk, headphones over tower; leave station as it was.

Assessment Strategies

- *Anecdotal observation*
- *Used internet correctly*
- *Tied class knowledge into project*
- *Saved 5 pictures to network*
- *Joined class discussion*

Trouble-shooting:
- *If there are tech problems, have students try to solve before you assist.*
- *You have print book and need website? Pick grade level and search (Alt+F) name on https://askatechteacher.wordpress.com/great-websites-for-kids/.*

Extension:
- *Here's a list of websites that discuss internet safety in second grade terms (no pdf? Use http://askatechteacher.wordpress.com/great-websites-for-kids/digital-citizenship/):*

  - *Internet Safety*
  - *Clicky's Netsmartz Kids*
  - *Cyberbullying—Garfield*
  - *Disney Surf Swell Island*

  - *Read-to-you book*
  - *My Online Neighborhood*
  - *Webonauts*

- *Full digital citizenship curriculum for K-8 available here. (http://www.structuredlearning.net/book/k-8-digital-citizenship-curriculum/).*
- *Offer websites that tie into class inquiry.*

- *Done? Create and print a St. Patrick's Day card without assistance (See sample inset). What's the purpose of greeting cards in technology:*

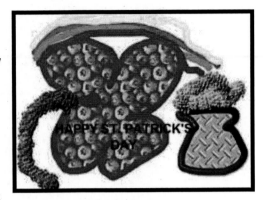

  - *Reinforce learned skills*
  - *Repetition is the key to learning*
  - *Students want to remember required skills to create artwork for parents*

- *Use SpellingCity.com to reinforce word study.*
- *Replace this lesson with Third Grade Lesson #4 How to Survive on Landforms in curriculum extendors (http://www.structuredlearning.net/book/k-6-curriculum-extender/).*

More Information:
- *Lesson questions? Go to http://askatechteacher.com*
- *Second grade teaching wiki: http://smaatechk-3.wikispaces.com/This+Week+in+Tech—Second+Grade*
- *PDF: See appendix for bonus websites*
- *Follow keyboard lessons in K-8 Keyboard Curriculum (http://ow.ly/j6GH8)*

If you don't get through everything, check completed items so you know what to get back to when you have time on later lessons. I find as I focus on the central idea of a lesson, clarifying questions sometimes take more time than I'd expect. I'm fine with that. There'll be lessons later that move faster than I planned.

"I sit looking at this computer screen all day long, day in and day out, week after week, and think: Man, if I could just find the 'on' switch..."

<u>Want to use this image?</u>

- Credit Kali Delamagente@ Ask a Tech Teacher
- Link back to her website if you share it digitally
- If it's not for educational use—DON'T USE IT. BUY IT!!

The law states that works of art created in the U.S. after January 1, 1978, are automatically protected by copyright once they are fixed in a tangible medium (like the internet) But a single copy may be used for scholarly research (even if that's a 2nd grade life cycle report) or in teaching or preparation to teach a class.

Netiquette Rules

- Be human
- Follow the same rules of behavior you follow in real life
- Be aware of your digital footprint
- Share your knowledge
- Help keep 'flame wars' under control
- Respect other's privacy
- Be forgiving of other's mistakes

Lesson #24—Report in MS Word I

Vocabulary	Problem solving	Big Idea
▥ Ctrl+enter ▥ Export ▥ Footer ▥ Handles ▥ Horizontal ▥ Insert ▥ Pound sign ▥ Tool ▥ Tool bar ▥ Vertical	▥ How do I start a new page (Ctrl+Enter) ▥ How do I resize a picture (use corner handles) ▥ How do I center vertically and horizontally? ▥ I can't see page number in footer (it's the pound sign) ▥ My text is greyed out (did you enter it in the footer?)	*Good writing requires editing and revising and guidance from teachers.*
Time Required *45 minutes*	**NETS-S Standards** *2b, 4a*	**CCSS** *CCSS.ELA-Literacy.W.2.5*

Essential Question

What elements make up good writing?

Overview

Materials

Internet, word processing program, drawing program, network folders

Teacher Preparation

- Talk with classroom teacher so you tie into their conversations about student reports
- Is class shorter than 45 minutes? Highlight the items most important to your integration with core classroom studies and leave the rest for 'later'

Steps

_____Continue classroom research/report. Open drawing program (i.e., KidPix, TuxPaint, Paint, or other). Draw a picture of animal being researched. This will be report cover (see inset). Use paint (or pencil) only—no stamps, stickers, backgrounds.

_____Export to network folder and close drawing program.

_____Discuss this personal drawing as it relates to pictures students copied from the internet last week. Now student is the artist. Would they want anyone to be able to take their picture for free? What are student thoughts on this. What if someone took student picture and sold it? What if picture was used to support a topic student disagreed with? Tie this into last week's discussions of image copyrights—it should make those conversations more personal. Take time so students can share their thoughts.

_____Open word processing program that allows for picture insert and formatting. We use Word. Quickly, review start page, tools, toolbars, ribbons, layout. Remind students of projects they completed using Word (maybe you have samples in classroom gallery).

_____Create a cover page for report by centering name of animal, student, teacher, vertically and horizontally. Use font 36, any font. Add picture student drew underneath. See top inset.

_____Add footer with student name and page. Explain footer as a way to keep info organized. Close footer. Ctrl+Enter for new page.

_____Begin typing on Page 2. Use font size 14, Times New Roman. Center and bold section titles; left-align sections; tab to start each section. This report has been edited with assistance of teacher, but help students refine writing conventions where necessary. When each section is typed, revise and edit, check grammar and spelling, smooth out sentence fluency, add formatting.

_____Remind students: Every time they use the computer, practice good keyboarding skills.

_____Insert animal picture from internet after each section. Be sure to center and resize to fit.

_____Remind students to transfer knowledge to classroom or home. This is particularly important in this project because students will do parts of report preparation in class or library. Remember skills used today!

_____Continually throughout class, check for understanding. Expect students to solve problems as they maneuver through lesson and make decisions that follow class rules.

_____As you teach, incorporate lesson vocabulary. Check this line if you did that today!

_____Save to network folder and close Word.

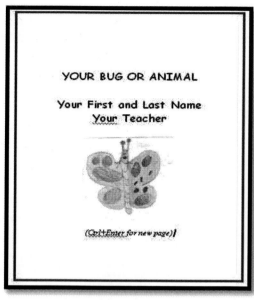

YOUR BUG OR ANIMAL

Your First and Last Name
Your Teacher

(Ctrl+Enter for new page)

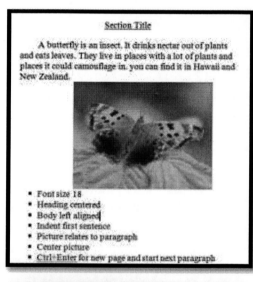

Section Title

A butterfly is an insect. It drinks nectar out of plants and eats leaves. They live in places with a lot of plants and places it could camouflage in. you can find it in Hawaii and New Zealand.

- Font size 18
- Heading centered
- Body left aligned
- Indent first sentence
- Picture relates to paragraph
- Center picture
- Ctrl+Enter for new page and start next paragraph

Assessment Strategies

- Completed cover page
- Began report body
- Found pics in network folder
- Joined class discussions
- Revised and edited report as required during typing

Trouble-shooting:

- _Didn't save images of all stages? Students can search for missing picture on internet (as done in prior lesson), then copy-paste directly into report._

- *Picture looks squashed (or skinny)? Remind student to resize only with corner handles.*
- *Hardware problems? Have students try to solve them before providing assistance.*
- *You have print book and need website? Pick grade level and search (Alt+F) name on https://askatechteacher.wordpress.com/great-websites-for-kids/.*

Extension:
- *Add a border to title page.*
- *Create cover in MS Publisher or an online tool like Big Huge Labs.*
- *Use kid-safe image websites included in article at end of lesson (Google for addresses if you have print book).*
- *Replace this lesson with 2ⁿᵈ Grade Lesson #3 How to Animoto curriculum extendors (http://www.structuredlearning.net/book/k-6-curriculum-extender/).*

More Information:
- *Lesson questions? Go to http://askatechteacher.com*
- *Second grade teaching wiki:*
  http://smaatechk-3.wikispaces.com/This+Week+in+Tech—Second+Grade
- *PDF: See appendix for bonus websites*
- *Follow keyboard lessons in K-8 Keyboard Curriculum (http://ow.ly/j6GH8)*

If you don't get through everything, check completed items so you know what to get back to when you have time on later lessons. I find as I focus on the central idea of a lesson, clarifying questions sometimes take more time than I'd expect. I'm fine with that. There'll be lessons later that move faster than I planned.

Font 36
Centered
Add your KP pic

Font 14
Align left
Double space
Add internet pics between sections that relate to sections

Dear Otto: Where Can I Find Kid-safe Images?

Dear Otto is an occasional column where I answer questions I get from readers about teaching tech. For privacy, I use only first names.

Here's a great question I got from a reader:

I am a computer lab teacher and teach grades 1-5. I can really use some advice from others. Do you have a good place for students to go and get images that are appropriate - I teach grades 1-5 and Google even with strict settings as well as MS Office clipart have some inappropriate images that come up from searches

This is harder than it should be. I use Google as a default because it is the safest of all the majors, not to say it's 100%. I spent quite a few hours one weekend checking out all of the kid-friendly child search engines (Sweet Search, KidSafe, QuinturaKids, Kigose, KidsClick, Ask Kids, KidRex, and more), but none did a good job filtering images. Content—yes, but images dried up to worthless for the needs of visual children.

So I went back to Google and tried their Safe Search settings. Normal Google search is set to moderate. For school age children, they can easily be set to Strict (check out this video on how to do it).

For some, even 'strict settings' isn't enough. Take the opportunity to teach students about internet safety, about what to do if they encounter something they shouldn't, about never straying from assigned websites. There's no way to protect children 100% from the world around them. Better we give them tools to survive and thrive, prepare them for the day we won't be there to protect their back.

For research websites for kids (beyond images), click here to go to my tech class internet start page. On the right side, if you scroll down, you'll see a box of links to good, solid kid-friendly websites.

Here's a list of kid-safe image websites. These are great, but limited in their content:

1. Creative Commons
2. Flikr—list restrictions— good learning tool
3. Free Photo
4. Google Life Project—from Life Mag
5. Morgue File—free, but check licenses
6. Open Clip Art
7. Open Photo
8. Pictures for Learning
9. Smithsonian Wild—200,000 of animals
10. Stock Exchange
11. Wiki Images

Lesson #25— Report in MS Word II

Vocabulary	Problem solving	Big Idea
▓ Alignment ▓ Back up ▓ Ctrl+Enter ▓ Cursor ▓ Double space ▓ Edit ▓ Flash drive ▓ Format ▓ Indent ▓ Start button ▓ Tab ▓ Word wrap	▓ Why can't I double space by pushing enter at end of a line? ▓ Double-space doesn't work (find toolbar tool) ▓ Indent doesn't work (use tab) ▓ What's the difference between backspace and delete? ▓ What's the difference between edit and format? ▓ How do I create a new page (Ctrl+Enter) ▓ Can't find file (Start-search)	*Good writing requires editing and revising and guidance from teachers.*
Time Required *45 minutes*	**NETS-S Standards** *3b, 4b*	**CCSS** *CCSS.ELA-Literacy.W.2.5*

Essential Question
What elements make up good writing?

Overview

Materials

Internet, word processing program, drawing program, network folders

Teacher Preparation

- Talk with classroom teacher so you tie into their conversations about student reports
- Have kid-safe image websites listed on class internet start page if required. Or have Google set to 'safe mode' if this is your approach
- Is class shorter than 45 minutes? Highlight the items most important to your integration with core classroom studies and leave the rest for 'later'.

Steps

_____Continue classroom report. This is week 3 of 4 on this project.

_____Start each paragraph with an indent (tab). Font size is 14, Times New Roman. Change line spacing to double space if desired.

_____Begin typing in font size 14, Times New Roman. Center and bold section titles; left-align sections; tab to start each section. Help students with writing conventions where necessary. When typing of each section is complete, revise and edit, check grammar and spelling, smooth out sentence fluency, add formatting.

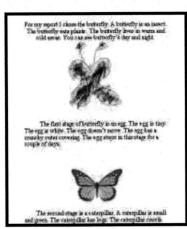

_____Remind students: Every time they use computer, practice good keyboarding.

_____To save, click 'X' and say 'yes'. This prevents confusion with 'save' and 'save as'. Back-up if available.

_____As you teach, remember to use correct vocabulary. Check this line item if you did that!

_____Continually throughout class, check for understanding. Expect students to solve problems as they maneuver through the lesson and make decisions that follow class rules.

_____Remind students to transfer knowledge to classroom or home.

_____Close down to desktop. Leave station with chair tucked under, etc.

Trouble-shooting:
- *Didn't save images of all stages? Students can search for missing picture on internet (as done in prior lesson), then copy-paste directly into report.*
- *Picture looks squashed (or skinny)? Resize only with corner handles.*
- *Hardware problems? Have students try to solve them before providing assistance.*
- *You have print book and need the website link? Search grade level. for name on https://askatechteacher.wordpress.com/great-websites-for-kids/.*

Extension:
- *If this lesson doesn't work for your student group, use one from **How to Jumpstart the Inquiry-based Classroom.** It has 5 projects aligned with SL curriculum.*

More Information:
- *Lesson questions? Go to http://askatechteacher.com*
- *Second grade teaching wiki: http://smaatechk-3.wikispaces.com/This+Week+in+Tech—Second+Grade*
- *PDF: See appendix for bonus websites*
- *Follow keyboard lessons in K-8 Keyboard Curriculum (http://ow.ly/j6GH8)*

If you don't get through everything, check completed items so you know what to get back to when you have time on later lessons. I find as I focus on the central idea of a lesson, clarifying questions sometimes take more time than I'd expect. I'm fine with that. There'll be lessons later that move faster than I planned.

"A printer consists of three main parts: the case, the jammed paper tray and the blinking red light"

-Anonymous

Lesson #26— Report in MS Word III

Vocabulary	Problem solving	Big Idea
▨ Ctrl+S ▨ Double space ▨ Font ▨ Grammar-check ▨ Indent ▨ Right-click ▨ Spell-check ▨ Tab ▨ Title page	▨ How do I save? (Ctrl+S) ▨ Can't find file (Start-search) ▨ Still lost? (Did you back up?) ▨ My typing disappeared? (Did you Ctrl+S every ten minutes?) ▨ Why can't I push enter at end of line to double space? ▨ Why can't I push spacebar to indent instead of tab?	*Good writing requires editing and revising and guidance from teachers.*

Time Required	NETS-S Standards	CCSS
45 minutes	*3b, 4b*	*CCSS.ELA-Literacy.W.2.5*

Essential Question
What elements make up good writing?

Overview

Materials

Internet, word processing program, drawing program, network folders

Teacher Preparation

- Talk with classroom teacher so you tie into conversations about student reports
- Have kid-safe image websites listed on class internet start page if required. Or have Google set to 'safe mode' if this is your approach
- Is class shorter than 45 minutes? Highlight items most important to your integration with core classroom studies and leave the rest for 'later'.

Steps

_____Continue classroom report. Start each paragraph with an indent (tab). Font size should be 14 (or what you decide). Change line spacing to double space; remember to tab at beginning of paragraph and don't push enter to wrap sentence (word processing program does it for you).

_____When done with report, revise and edit as needed.

_____Remind students: Every time they use the computer, practice good keyboarding skills.

_____Remember Ctrl+S—every 10 minutes.

_____As you teach, include lesson vocab. Check this line if you did that today!

The animal am researching is the chicken. My animal is a bird. The chicken eats insects, seeds, grass, table scraps, potatoes and bread. The chicken lives in a henhouse and a chicken coop. The temperature my animal lives in is 95 degrees Fahrenheit. Usually you find chickens all around the world in farms. My animal is most active during the day.

Phase 1 of the life cycle!
My animal begins as an egg. The egg is two inches long and is approximately two ounces. The egg is tan and brown. The outer covering of the egg is hard. It helps protect the animal by its hard, outer shell. The egg stays in this stage for a few months.

The second stage of the chicken is the chick. The chick has yellow feathers with an orange beak and fluffy feathers. The chick has two wings and two legs. Covering of the

_____Continually throughout class, check for understanding. Expect students to solve problems as they maneuver through the lesson and make decisions that follow class rules.

_____Remind students to transfer knowledge to classroom or home.

_____Exit with Alt+F4. Tuck chairs under desk, headphones over tower; leave station as you found it.

Assessment Strategies

- *Completed project*
- *Revised and edited as needed*
- *Transferred knowledge to other classes/everyday life*

Trouble-shooting:

- *Hardware problems? Have students try to solve them before providing assistance.*
- *You have the print book and need the website link? Visit https://askatechteacher.wordpress.com/great-websites-for-kids/. Pick the grade level. Search (Alt+F) for the name.*

Extension:

- *Students work with neighbor to revise and edit each other's work.*
- *Offer additional websites on subjects that tie into class conversation.*
- *If this lesson doesn't work for your student group, use one from **How to Jumpstart the Inquiry-based Classroom.** It has 5 additional projects aligned with the SL curriculum.*

More Information:

- *Lesson questions? Go to http://askatechteacher.com*
- *Second grade teaching wiki: http://smaatechk-3.wikispaces.com/This+Week+in+Tech—Second+Grade*
- *PDF: See appendix for bonus websites*
- *Follow keyboard lessons in K-8 Keyboard Curriculum (http://ow.ly/j6GH8)*

If you don't get through everything, check completed items so you know what to get back to when you have time on later lessons. I find as I focus on the central idea of a lesson, clarifying questions sometimes take more time than I'd expect. I'm fine with that. There'll be lessons later that move faster than I planned.

"hAS aNYONE sEEN MY cAPSLOCK kEY ?"

Lesson #27—Intro to PowerPoint

Vocabulary	Problem solving	Big Idea
▓ Editors ▓ Multimedia ▓ PowerPoint ▓ Ribbon ▓ Slide ▓ Slide show ▓ Subtitle ▓ Task pane	▓ Program disappeared (check taskbar) ▓ Computer broken (Did you push power on CPU or monitor?) ▓ No task pane (check 'view') ▓ Can't find PowerPoint on computer (Start>search)	*Good writing requires editing and revising and guidance from teachers*
Time Required *45 minutes*	**NETS-S Standards** *3b, 4b*	**CCSS** *CCSS.ELA-Literacy.W.2.6*

Essential Question
What elements make up good writing?

Overview

Materials

Internet, slideshow program

Teacher Preparation

- Have slideshows from last year's 2nd graders available
- Talk with classroom teacher so you tie into conversations about student reports
- Is class shorter than 45 minutes? Highlight the items most important to your integration with core classroom studies and leave the rest for 'later'

Steps

_____Warm up with keyboarding on software or online program.

_____Explain PowerPoint. It's a dynamic approach to sharing student's interdisciplinary array of skills, the 21st Century storybook told not just with words, but color, movement, dazzling layout and sound. It allows for differentiation of instruction. All types of learners shine as they share their knowledge with slideshows.

_____Students will prepare a 'movie' of this year's work to share with parents. Remember last year's slideshow? This will be more authentic in its assessment of knowledge.

_____Show slideshows by last year's 2nd graders. Turn lights off to enhance the experience.

_____Discuss differences students noticed between PowerPoint and Word projects completed this year. What stood out? What would they use PowerPoint for? How about Word? Extend conversation to include likes/dislikes of both programs.

_____Open PowerPoint. Review screen layout—slides on left, slide being worked on in middle, task pane on right, ribbon at top.

_____Click to add title—'My Story'; click to add subtitle—'student name'.

_____Add five slides. Watch them populate on left. That's a total of six slides—one for cover, four for pictures, one to close.

_____As you teach, include lesson vocab. Check this line if you did that today!

_____Throughout class, check for understanding. Expect students to solve problems as they maneuver through the lesson and make decisions that follow class rules.

_____Remind students to transfer this knowledge to the classroom or home.

_____Save to student network folder using student last name as part of file name. Tuck chairs under desk, headphones over tower; leave station as you found it.

Assessment Strategies
- *Completed cover*
- *Followed instructions*
- *Joined class discussion*

Trouble-shooting:
- *When students have difficulty doing what you teach, ask why. And listen. You may be surprised by the answer.*
- *You have print book and need website? Pick grade level and search (Alt+F) name on https://askatechteacher.wordpress.com/great-websites-for-kids/.*

Extension:
- *Offer additional websites on subjects that tie into class conversation.*
- *If this lesson doesn't work for your student group, use one from **How to Jumpstart the Inquiry-based Classroom.** It has 5 additional projects aligned with SL curriculum.*

More Information:
- *Lesson questions? Go to http://askatechteacher.com*
- *Second grade teaching wiki:*
  http://smaatechk-3.wikispaces.com/This+Week+in+Tech—Second+Grade
- *PDF: See appendix for bonus websites*
- *Follow keyboard lessons in K-8 Keyboard Curriculum (http://ow.ly/j6GH8)*

If you don't get through everything, check completed items so you know what to get back to when you have time on later lessons. I find as I focus on the central idea of a lesson, clarifying questions sometimes take more time than I'd expect. I'm fine with that. There'll be lessons later that move faster than I planned.

Lesson #28—PowerPoint Basics I

Vocabulary	Problem solving	Big Idea
▪ Design ▪ Drill down ▪ Handles ▪ Image ▪ Network ▪ PowerPoint ▪ Right-click ▪ Slide show ▪ Software ▪ Task pane ▪ Tool bar	▪ I can't find my project (where did you save it? Look in 'My Documents'. Search with 'Search' tool) ▪ Where is period? (by question mark) ▪ How do I capitalize? (Use shift for one letter, caps for all) ▪ Picture got weird (only use corner handles to resize) ▪ Can't find right picture (use any picture in your folder; make slide title match)	*Technology provides a variety of methods to communicate my ideas*
Time Required *45 minutes*	**NETS-S Standards** 2b, 6a	**CCSS** *CCSS.ELA-Literacy.W.2.6*

Essential Question
I'm not a writer. Can I still communicate my ideas?

Overview

Materials

Internet, slideshow program, network folders (with student pictures)

Teacher Preparation
- Talk with classroom teacher so you tie into their conversations
- Is class shorter than 45 minutes? Highlight items most important to your integration with core classroom studies and leave the rest for 'later'

Steps

_____Warm up with keyboarding on software or online program. Remind students of good habits—hands curled over home row, elbows at sides, keyboard in front of body.

_____With PowerPoint, expect students to minimize text focus and maximize design, layout, pictures, colors as methods of communicating ideas. You can use other presentation software (Google Docs, Open Office), but PowerPoint has the easiest and most complete set of tools to enable an age-appropriate student-centered project for second graders.

_____Remind students: This is one of many digital tools they have used this year to advance education.

_____Have students open projects saved last week. If they can't find them, 1) check My Documents, 2) search using their last name.

_____Pick a 'Design' from menu to be used as background on all slides.

_____Select Slide #2 on left sidebar. See how it shows in middle of screen? Insert first picture to be used. Show students how to drill down to their network folder to find an image.

_____Resize by grabbing corner handles and moving toward center.

_____Add title at top that summarizes what picture is/says. Repeat on three more slides with three more pictures from network folder.

_____Ctrl+S to save to student folder every 10 minutes. Use 'x' in upper right corner to close. Why use 'x' instead of 'save'? It will save project where student opened it.

_____As you teach, use lesson vocab. Check this line if you did that today!

_____Continually throughout class, check for understanding. Expect students to solve problems as they maneuver through the lesson and make decisions that follow class rules.

_____Remind students to transfer knowledge to the classroom or home.

_____Tuck chairs under desk, headphones over tower; leave station as you found it.

Assessment Strategies
- Anecdotal observation
- Followed directions
- Saved correctly

Trouble-shooting:
- _Student can't find one of their pictures? Use a different one._
- _Student has more than four pictures? Use any four they want._
- _You have print book and need website? Pick grade level and search (Alt+F) name on https://askatechteacher.wordpress.com/great-websites-for-kids/._

Extension:
- _Allow students who finish to add more pictures to slideshow._
- _Differentiate design for slide backgrounds. Select a slide, right-click a design on ribbon, and 'add to selected slide'._
- _Offer websites on subjects that tie into class inquiry._
- _If this lesson doesn't work for your students, use one from **How to Jumpstart the Inquiry-based Classroom.** It has 5 projects aligned with SL curriculum._

More Information:
- _Lesson questions? Go to http://askatechteacher.com_
- _Second grade teaching wiki:_
  http://smaatechk-3.wikispaces.com/This+Week+in+Tech—Second+Grade
- _PDF: See appendix for bonus websites_
- _Follow keyboard lessons in K-8 Keyboard Curriculum (http://ow.ly/j6GH8)_

If you don't get through everything, check completed items so you know what to get back to when you have time on later lessons. I find as I focus on the central idea of a lesson, clarifying questions sometimes take more time than I'd expect. I'm fine with that. There'll be lessons later that move faster than I planned.

Lesson #29—PowerPoint Basics II

Vocabulary	Problem solving	Big Idea
▪ *Animation* ▪ *Drill down* ▪ *Flash drive* ▪ *Handles* ▪ *Menu bar* ▪ *My documents* ▪ *Resize* ▪ *Ribbon* ▪ *Scheme* ▪ *Software*	▪ *Double-click doesn't work (push enter)* ▪ *What's the difference between software and an internet tool?* ▪ *I can't find my project (where did you save it?)* ▪ *I can't remember where I saved (use Search under Start button)* ▪ *How do I keep 'animation' on slide (once clicked, it's there)*	*Technology provides a variety of methods to communicate ideas*
Time Required *45 minutes*	**NETS-S Standards** *2b, 6a*	**CCSS** *CCSS.ELA-Literacy.W.2.6*

Essential Question

How can technology communicate my ideas better than other ways?

Overview

Materials

Internet, slideshow program

Teacher Preparation

- Talk with classroom teacher so you tie into their conversations
- Is class shorter than 45 minutes? Highlight items most important to your integration with core classroom studies and leave the rest for 'later'.

Steps

_____Warm up with keyboarding on software or online program. Remind students of good habits—hands curled over home row, elbows at sides, keyboard I front of body.

_____Before beginning: Ask students what digital tool they are using. What does that mean? Why use PowerPoint and not paper and pencil?

_____The focus of 2nd grade PowerPoint is understanding software so students can use it facilely in later grades for formative and summative assignments.

_____Have student open project saved last week. If s/he can't find it, 1) check My Documents, 2) search using their last name.

_____Finish adding pictures from student folder until four slides are completed. Resize as needed.

_____Click to add title. Create a title that sums up intent of picture.

_____Last slide will have title, 'The End'

_____Remind students to Ctrl+S every ten minutes.

_____Click on slide #1 (in left sidebar).Go to 'Animation'. Explain what this means and show examples. Have students animate only title of slide. Animate next five slides.

_____As you teach, use correct vocabulary. Check this line if you did that today!

_____Continually throughout class, check for understanding. Expect students to solve problems as they maneuver through the lesson and make decisions that follow class rules.

_____Remind students to transfer this knowledge to classroom or home.

_____Tuck chairs under desk, headphones over tower; leave station as you found it.

Assessment Strategies
- *Anecdotal observation*
- *Transferred knowledge to other classes/everyday life*

Trouble-shooting:
- *No title box on slide? Picture is probably covering it. Resize to reveal where title box should be.*
- *Hardware problems? Have students try to solve before providing assistance.*
- *You have print book and need website? Pick grade level and search (Alt+F) name on https://askatechteacher.wordpress.com/great-websites-for-kids/.*
- *Student can't find project? Search using Start>search. Hint: Never resave with 'save-as'. Often, file ends up in wrong place.*

Extension:
- *Have students review each other's slideshows and make suggestions.*
- *Offer websites on internet start page that tie into class conversation.*
- *If this lesson doesn't work for your student group, use one from **How to Jumpstart the Inquiry-based Classroom.** It has 5 additional projects aligned with SL curriculum.*

More Information:
- *Lesson questions? Go to http://askatechteacher.com*
- *Second grade teaching wiki:*
  http://smaatechk-3.wikispaces.com/This+Week+in+Tech—Second+Grade
- *Follow keyboard lessons in K-8 Keyboard Curriculum (http://ow.ly/j6GH8)*

If you don't get through everything, check completed items so you know what to get back to when you have time on later lessons. I find as I focus on the central idea of a lesson, clarifying questions sometimes take more time than I'd expect. I'm fine with that. There'll be lessons later that move faster than I planned.

Lesson #30—PowerPoint Basics III

Vocabulary	Problem solving	Big Idea
🖳 *Animation* 🖳 *Auto-advance* 🖳 *Edit* 🖳 *Format* 🖳 *Mouse click* 🖳 *Save as* 🖳 *Trans-* 🖳 *Transition*	🖳 *My computer doesn't work (is power on?)* 🖳 *My monitor doesn't work (is power on?)* 🖳 *What's the difference between 'save' and 'save as'?* 🖳 *What's the difference between 'format' and 'edit'?*	***Technology provides a variety of methods to communicate my ideas***
Time Required *45 minutes*	**NETS-S Standards** *2b, 6a*	**CCSS** *CCSS.ELA-Literacy.W.2.6*

Essential Question

How can technology communicate my ideas better than other ways?

Overview

Materials

Internet, slideshow program

Teacher Preparation

* Experiment with online slideshow programs to see if you can use them to share student projects
* Talk with classroom teacher so you tie into their conversations
* Is class shorter than 45 minutes? Highlight items most important to your integration with core classroom studies and leave the rest for 'later'.

Steps

_____Warm up with keyboarding on installed software or online program. Remind students of good habits—hands curled over home row, elbows at sides, keyboard I front of body.

_____The focus of 2nd grade PowerPoint is understanding software so students can use it later for class formative and summative assignments. Other presentation software (Google Docs, Open Office) will work also, but PowerPoint has the easiest and most complete set of tools to enable an age-appropriate student-centered project.

_____Have student open project saved last week. If s/he can't find it, 1) check My Documents, 2) search using their last name.

_____Go to 'Transition'. Discuss what it is. Compare it to other words with prefix 'trans-'.

_____Add three items:

- o *Transition between slides--slow*
- o *Speed of transition*
- o *Auto-advance*

_____Repeat for each slide.

_____Remind students to Ctrl+S every ten minutes.

_____Final step: add two pictures to each slide, one that moves and one that doesn't:

- *Add non-moving picture with clipart. Search for topic that fits slide*
- *Add moving picture via 'movie'*

_____Have GIFs (aka movies) suited to class topics in a network folder. Here's a collection (http://askatechteacher.wordpress.com/great-websites-for-kids/animated-gifs/) I use.

_____Done with everything? Pair up with a neighbor and fill out rubric checklist (see next pages) on each other's slideshow. Help with editing, formatting, and all required items. Present slideshow to each other in preparation for class presentation. Try to talk without reading slide and fitting all information in time allotted (approx. five seconds).

_____Close to desktop. Why shouldn't students 'save-as' (only for a new name or location).

_____As you teach, use lesson vocab. Check this line item if you did that today!

_____Continually throughout class, check for understanding. Expect students to solve problems as they maneuver through the lesson and make decisions that follow class rules.

_____Remind students to transfer knowledge to classroom or home.

_____Tuck chairs under desk, headphones over tower; leave station as you found it.

Assessment Strategies
- *Worked well with partner*
- *Completed project*
- *Completed rubric*
- *Understood use of 'digital tools'*

Trouble-shooting:
- *GIF doesn't move? Push Shift+F7 to watch slide it's in.*
- *You have print book and need the website link? Pick grade level from this website https://askatechteacher.wordpress.com/great-websites-for-kids/. Search (Alt+F) name.*

Extension:
- *Upload to Slideboom, Slideshare, or other online tool to share with school community (Google for links).*
- *Offer additional websites on subjects that tie into class conversation.*

- If this lesson doesn't work for your student group, use one from **_How to Jumpstart the Inquiry-based Classroom._** It has 5 projects aligned with the SL curriculum.

More Information:
- *Lesson questions? Go to http://askatechteacher.com*
- *Second grade teaching wiki: http://smaatechk-3.wikispaces.com/This+Week+in+Tech—Second+Grade*
- *PDF: See appendix for bonus websites*
- *Follow keyboard lessons in K-8 Keyboard Curriculum (http://ow.ly/j6GH8)*

If you don't get through everything, check completed items so you know what to get back to when you have time on later lessons. I find as I focus on the central idea of a lesson, clarifying questions sometimes take more time than I'd expect. I'm fine with that. There'll be lessons later that move faster than I planned.

Is Windows a virus?

No, Windows is not a virus. Here's what viruses do:

1. **They replicate quickly** - *okay, Windows does that.*
2. **Viruses use up valuable system resources, slowing down the system as they do so** - *okay, Windows does that.*
3. **Viruses will, from time to time, trash your hard disk** - *okay, Windows does that too.*
4. **Viruses are usually carried, unknown to the user, along with valuable programs and systems.** - *Sigh.. Windows does that, too.*
5. **Viruses will occasionally make the user suspect their system is out of date and the user will buy new hardware.** - *Yup, Windows does that, too.*

But there are fundamental differences: Viruses are well supported by their authors, are running on most systems, their program code is fast, compact and efficient and they tend to become more sophisticated as they mature.

So Windows is not a virus.

It's a bug.

POWERPOINT GRADING RUBRIC

Name_____   Teacher_____

Here's a list of required skills in your PowerPoint project. Check off those that you've included. Then, add those that you've missed. When you're done, turn in the grading rubric and I'll grade your project.

1. Cover slide   _____

2. The end slide with your picture   _____

3. Each slide has title   _____

4. Each slide has KidPix picture   _____

5. Each slide has clip art and GIF   _____

6. No spelling/grammar errors   _____

7. Animations   _____

8. Transitions   _____

9. Slides auto-advance   _____

10. Class presentation   _____

    a. Face audience   _____

    b. Talk to audience   _____

    c. Introduce yourself   _____

    d. Speak loud enough   _____

    e. No 'umms' or stuttering   _____

Lesson #31—Father's Day Greetings

Vocabulary	Problem solving	Big Idea
▨ *Animations* ▨ *Esc* ▨ *GIF* ▨ *Movie* ▨ *Shift+F5*	▨ *Screen froze (is task bar blinking?)* ▨ *Can't find project (Where did you save it?)* ▨ *Can't exit program (try Alt+F4)*	*I can use technology to make stuff I use at home*

Time Required	NETS-S Standards	CCSS
45 minutes	*2b, 6a*	*CCSS.ELA-Literacy.W.2.6*

Essential Question
Can I use technology at home for stuff that isn't about school?

Overview

Materials

Internet, slideshow program, network folders, drawing program, printer

Teacher Preparation
- Is class shorter than 45 minutes? Highlight the items most important to your integration with core classroom studies and leave the rest for 'later'.

Steps

_____Finish anything not completed on slideshow. This is an overflow day. Use rubric with a partner to review and complete.

_____Finished? Make a Father's Day card in KidPix, Publisher or Word. This is self-directed. Use Ctrl+S to save every 10 minutes; print.

_____As you teach, use lesson vocab. Check this line if you did that today!

_____Continually throughout class, check for understanding. Expect students to solve problems as they maneuver through the lesson and make decisions that follow class rules.

_____Remind students to transfer knowledge to the classroom or home.

_____Close to desktop using Alt+F4; tuck chairs under desk, headphones over tower; leave station as you found it.

Assessment Strategies
- *Anecdotal observation*
- *Completed project*
- *Transferred knowledge to other classes/everyday life*

Trouble-shooting:

- *You have the print book and need the website link? Pick grade level from this website https://askatechteacher.wordpress.com/great-websites-for-kids/. Search (Alt+F) name.*

Extension:
- *Upload to Slideboom, Slideshare, or other online tool to share with school community.*
- *Offer additional websites on subjects that tie into class conversation.*
  Replace lesson with 2nd Grade lesson #4 Big Huge Labs Those Pictures! in curriculum extendors (http://www.structuredlearning.net/book/k-6-curriculum-extender/).
- *Replace lesson with 2nd Grade Lesson #4 Big Huge Labs Those Pictures! in curriculum extendors (http://www.structuredlearning.net/book/k-6-curriculum-extender/).*

More Information:
- *Lesson questions? Go to http://askatechteacher.com*
- *Second grade teaching wiki:*
  http://smaatechk-3.wikispaces.com/This+Week+in+Tech—Second+Grade
- *PDF: See appendix for bonus websites*
- *Follow keyboard lessons in K-8 Keyboard Curriculum (http://ow.ly/j6GH8)*

If you don't get through everything, check completed items so you know what to get back to when you have time on later lessons. I find as I focus on the central idea of a lesson, clarifying questions sometimes take more time than I'd expect. I'm fine with that. There'll be lessons later that move faster than I planned.

Disney Password

My kids love going to the Web, and they keep track of their passwords by writing them on Post-it notes.

I asked why their Disney password was so long— "MickeyMinnieGoofyPluto,".

"Because," my son explained, "they say it has to have at least four characters."

Lesson #32—Endings and Beginnings

Vocabulary	Problem solving	Big Idea
• *Digital tools*	• *Can't find slideshow (search by last name)*	*I know more than I think I do*
Time Required 45 minutes	**NETS-S Standards** 6d	**CCSS** Anchor

Essential Question
What have I learned this year?

Overview

Materials

Internet, student slideshows, SmartScreen, popcorn?

Teacher Preparation
- Test equipment so everything works well for parent show
- Make sure all student slideshows are in their folders

Steps

_____Share slideshows on SmartScreen. Each student describes their drawings and key details they feel important. Answer parent questions to clarify.

_____Award certificates (see sample, end of text).

_____Done? Share websites from start page.

_____Tuck chairs under, headphones over tower; leave station as it was. Have a great summer!

Assessment Strategies
- *Anecdotal*

Trouble-shooting:
- *You have print book and need website link? Search (Alt+F) name at https://askatechteacher.wordpress.com/great-websites-for-kids/.*

Extension:
- *Let students draw anything they'd like in KidPix, to be printed for parents*

More Information:
- *Lesson questions? Go to http://askatechteacher.com*
- *Second grade teaching wiki:*
  http://smaatechk-3.wikispaces.com/This+Week+in+Tech—Second+Grade
- *PDF: See appendix for bonus websites*

> *"As a computer, I find your faith in technology amusing."*

PS

If you teach technology, it's likely you're a geek. Even if you didn't start out that way–say, you used to be a first grade teacher and suddenly your Admin in their infinite wisdom, moved you to the tech lab—you became a geek. You morphed into the go-to person for tech problems, computer quirks, crashes and freezes.

Overnight, your colleagues assumed you received an upload of data that allowed you to Know the answers to their every techie question. It didn't matter that yesterday, you were one of them. Now, you are on a pedestal, their necks craned upward as they ask you, *How do I get the SmartScreen to work?* or *We need the microphones working for a lesson I'm starting in three minutes. Can you please-please-please fix them?*

Celebrate your cheeky geekiness. Flaunt it for students and colleagues. Play Minecraft. That's you now–you are sharp, quick-thinking. You tingle when you see an iPad. You wear a flash drive like jewelry. The first thing you do when you get to school is check your email

It's OK. Here at Structured Learning and Ask a Tech Teacher, we understand. The readers understand. You're at home. To honor you, we've created these two posters (see next pages). They provide more ways to get your geek fully on as you go through your day.

10 steps To become A BETTER GEEK

1. Use **Tech**
2. Use **it** every day--save some trees
3. Use **it** when it seems difficult
4. Use **it** in class--and at home
5. Use **Tech** now--right now
6. Use **it** instead of something else
7. Teach a friend to use **it**
8. Teach a lot of friends to use **it**
9. Make **it** your first choice
10. Keep using **it**

15 ways To GET YOUR GEEK ON

1. Be smart. Yeah, it feels good
2. That's my inner Geek speaking
3. Think. Exercise your brain.
4. Waves. Sigh.
5. Keep repeating, *People are my friends*. Like Siri.
6. Move away from the keyboard--Not.
7. Some people watch TV. I play with a Rubik's Cube
8. Be patient. I'm buffering.
9. There must be a shortkey for that
10. Life needs an Undo key
11. Leave me alone for 2 minutes and I'll go to sleep
12. Yes, I can fix your computer
13. Like a computer, I do what you tell me to
14. My RAM is full. Come back later.
15. Slow down. My processor isn't that fast

INTERNET SITES

Visit the <u>Ask a Tech Teacher</u> website for links and updates (http://askatechteacher.com). If you have a digital copy of this book, Ctrl+click to access links below.

Please be aware: Links are constantly changing. Let us know if you find one that requires an update!

Animals

1. Animal Adaptations
2. Animal Games
3. Animal Games II
4. Animal homes
5. Animal Homes III
6. Animals
7. Classify animals
8. Endangered species collection
9. Food Chains
10. Habitats—create one
11. Habitats—match them
12. Life Cycles
13. Ocean Currents—video from NASA
14. Ocean Safari
15. Ocean Tracks

Art

1. Art—Make a monster
2. Create bomomos, Mondrian, etc.
3. Drawminos
4. Metropolitan Museum of Art
5. Minneapolis Institute of Arts
6. Mr. Picassa Head
7. Museum of Modern Art
8. National Gallery of Art—for kids
9. Sistine Chapel

Counting Coins and Money

1. Brain Pop Learn about Money
2. Cash Out
3. Coin Counting
4. Coin games—from US Mint
5. Count Money
6. Counting Money
7. Face on money
8. How much money
9. Make change
10. Money—counting
11. Moneyville
12. Pick A Coin
13. Piggy Bank
14. US Mint virtual tour (a slideshow)
15. World of Money—registration required

Culture

1. Google World of Wonders
2. 360 Panorama of the world

Digital Citizenship

1. Badguy Patrol
2. Chatting online
3. Clicky's internet safety
4. Disney's Surf Swell Island
5. Faux Paws Internet Safety
6. Garfield internet safety
7. Hector's World Internet safety videos
8. Internet—what is it—video

9. Internet safety
10. Internet safety Dance Video
11. Internet safety video—day in digcit's life
12. Internet safety videos
13. Internet safety—BrainPop Jr
14. Internet Smart Princess
15. Netiquette online

16. Popups
17. Private info online
18. Safe Search—Kigose
19. Safety Land—with certificate at end
20. Who are your online friends?

Ecology

1. Eco-friendly house
2. Eeko World
3. Breathing earth— the environment

4. Conservation Game
5. Home of the Future
6. My Garbology

Economics

1. Brain Pop Learn about Money
2. Coffee Shop Game
3. Ump

4. Various Econ sites I
5. Various Econ sites II

Geography

1. Forest—Walk Through a Forest
2. Geography—find letters around the world
3. Geogreeting—find letters around the world
4. Learn the states
5. Maps—fun game from NG
6. Maps—more games from NG
7. Rainforest—3 games

8. Rainforest—Jungle Journey
9. Rainforest—great but a bit of reading
10. Rainforest collection
11. Rainforest Websites Videos
12. USA Puzzle
13. Virtual tours

Greece-Rome

1. Ancient Rome—Winged Sandals
2. Archaeology Game
3. Egyptians Madlibs
4. Greeks—Primary grades

5. Pharaoh's Tomb
6. Starfall Greek Myths
7. Winged Sandals

Holidays

1. Earth Day
2. Groundhog Day Games

3. Groundhog Day Videos

Holiday—Christmas

1. Holidays around the world
2. Holiday Crossword
3. Holiday—North Pole Academy
4. Holiday—find the word
5. Holiday—Math Facts

6. Holiday music
7. Holiday Elf Games
8. Holiday—Design Gingerbread House
9. Holiday—match game
10. Holiday music

11. Santa Tracker

Holidays—St. Patrick's Day

1. Coloring Pages
2. Color the shamrock
3. Color the Pot-o-gold
4. Color the leprechaun
5. Coloring—More coloring pages
6. Coloring—More coloring pages
7. Games—St. Pat's games and activities
8. Puzzle—St. Pat's Puzzle
9. Puzzle—St. Pat's puzzle II
10. Puzzle—St. Pat's drag-and-drop puzzle
11. Puzzle—St. Pat's slide puzzle
12. Puzzle—St. Pat's slide puzzle II
13. Puzzle—St. Pat's greeting—in a puzzle
14. Puzzle—Leprechaun jigsaw puzzle
15. Quiz—St. Patrick's Day Quiz
16. St. Pat's math
17. St. Patrick's Day history—video
18. St. Pat's Day songs—video
19. St. Pat's Sudoku
20. Tic tac toe
21. Webquest for St. Patrick's Day I
22. Webquest II
23. Wordsearch
24. Webquest III

Holidays—Valentines

1. Valentine Sudoku
2. Valentine mouse skills
3. Line up the hearts
4. Dress up the heart
5. Valentine unscramble
6. Valentine typing
7. Valentine puppy jigsaw
8. Valentine drag-and-drop
9. Valentine match
10. Valentine tic-tac-toe
11. Valentine projects from Winter Wonderland
12. Write in a heart
13. More heart writing
14. 'I love you' in languages Afrikaans to Zulu
15. Valentine's Day apps
16. Valentine Day games and stories
17. Valentine coloring book
18. Valentine Day poem generator
19. Valentine rebuses
20. Valentine rebus game

Human Body

1. Blood Flow
2. Body Systems
3. Brain Pop—Body—UN smaa PW techclass
4. Build a Skeleton
5. Build a Skeleton II
6. Can you place these parts in the correct place?
7. Choose the systems you want to see.
8. Find My Body Parts
9. Google Human Body
10. Health games
11. Health Games—BrainPop
12. Heart Trek—Be the beat
13. How the body works—videos
14. Human body—interactive
15. Human Body Games
16. Human Body websites
17. Human Body Websites II
18. Human Body—by a 2nd grade class—video
19. Human Body—videos on how body parts work
20. Inside the Human Body: Grades 1-3
21. Keep Ben Healthy
22. Kid's Bio—Human Body
23. Kids' Health-My Body
24. Label the body
25. Matching Senses
26. Mr. Bones—put his body together
27. Muscles Game
28. Nutrition Music and Games from Dole
29. Senses Challenge
30. Weird stuff your body does

Internet Safety

1. Avatar—Clay yourself
2. Avatar 1—a monster
3. Avatar 2—Lego you
4. Avatar 3—animal
5. Avatar 4—make me a hero
6. Avatar 5—MadMen yourself
7. Avatar 6—Voki yourself
8. Internet safety
9. Safety Land—with certificate at end

Keyboarding Practice

1. Alphabet rain game
2. Barracuda game
3. Bubbles game
4. Finger jig practice game
5. Free typing tutor
6. Keyboard challenge—grade level
7. Keyboard practice—quick start
8. Keyboard test—quick, adjustable
9. Keyboarding for Kids
10. Keyboarding practice
11. Keyboarding resources listed
12. Keyboarding—alphabet rain game
13. Keyboarding—barracuda game
14. Keyboarding—bubbles game
15. Keyboarding—Dance Mat Typing
16. Keyboarding—full online course
17. Keyboarding—games
18. Keyboarding—lessons
19. Keyboarding—lessons and speed quiz
20. Keyboarding—more lessons
21. Keyboarding—must sign up, but free
22. Keyboarding—quick start
23. Keyboarding—speed quiz
24. Keyboard—practice with a game
25. Krazy keyboarding for kids
26. Learn to Type—Big Brown Bear
27. Online practice
28. Online typing course
29. Online typing lessons
30. Online typing lessons — even more
31. Online typing lessons — more
32. TuxTyping
33. Typing—Brown Bear
34. Typing Defense—fun word practice
35. Typing program—a graduated course

Languages

1. Babbel.com
2. Busuu.com
3. Live Mocha
4. Mango Languages

Language Arts

1. Adjectives and nouns—matching
2. Adjective Game
3. BiteSize—Reading, Writing, Grammar
4. Grammar Blast
5. Grammar games
6. Grammaropolis
7. Math/LA Videos by grade level
8. Nouns Rock
9. Poems in shapes—fun
10. Vocabulary Fun

Life Cycle

1. Lifecycles
2. Plant life cycle
3. Frog life cycle
4. Life cycle—Bitesize
5. Life cycle of a frog—scroll to Ch 2
6. Life cycle of a snake
7. Life Cycle Videos

Literacy

Games—Brainpop

Math

1. A Plus Math
2. Alien Addition
3. Cool Math for Kids
4. Count us in—variety of math practice
5. Game-oriented math learning
6. HoodaMath
7. Interactive Math Web Lessons for Grades 2-6
8. Internet links for 2nd grade—a bunch for math
9. Learn Multiplication facts—the fun way
10. Links, by math topic—some for speed math
11. Math Basics
12. Math Concepts—games, etc.
13. Math—Grids
14. Math Grids II
15. Math links by skills
16. Math Playground
17. Math practice—by skill and length of time
18. Math Practice Test
19. Math skills links
20. Math—by Grade Level—lots of stuff
21. Math Games
22. Math/LA Videos by grade level
23. Math—Wild on Math—simple to use
24. Mental Math Drills
25. More Quick Math
26. Multiflier math practice
27. Multiplication Tables
28. Number Nut Math Games
29. Ones, tens, hundreds
30. Quick Math
31. Quick Math II
32. Quick Math—by level
33. Simulations—varied
34. Speed Math
35. SumDog—free reg
36. Test Your Math
37. Virtual Manipulatives and Tessellations
38. Wild on Math—simple to use
39. Word and logic problems
40. XtraMath—free but reg

Miscellaneous

1. Biographies
2. Chess
3. Edutainment with BBC
4. Games that make you think
5. Graphic organizers—Enchanted Learning
6. Great Websites—can't get thru all of them
7. Heroes—kids who are heroes
8. Logic games
9. Puzzle of student pic—create
10. Quick quizzes—how much do you know?
11. School Tube—organized by topics

Music

1. Beat Lab
2. Carnegie Hall
3. Classical KUSC
4. Classics for Kids
5. Create Music
6. Dallas Symphony Orchestra for Kid
7. Jake the Philharmonic Dog
8. Music Games

9. Music with hands
10. Nashville Symphony
11. National Jukebox
12. New York Philharmonic Kidzone

13. Play Music
14. Quincy and the Magic Instruments
15. San Francisco Symphony Kids Sites

Pictures

12. Google Life Project—from Life Mag
13. Pictures for Learning

14. Smithsonian Wild—200k animal pics!

Plants
Plant life cycle

Poetry

1. Fill-in-the-blank poetry—easy and hard
2. Fill-in-the-blank poems

3. Giggle Poetry
4. Poetry Engine—writes poem for you

Reading
Reading games

Research

1. Ask Kids
2. Brain Pop
3. How Stuff Works
4. Kid Rex
5. Kids Click
6. Kid's Konnect
7. Kid's Research
8. Kids Konnect

9. Kids Research
10. Pics for Learning
11. QuinteraKids—visual Search engine
12. Safe Search—Kigose
13. Sweet Search
14. World Book Online

Science

1. 3D Toad—3D science study
2. Amazing 3D world—via skateboard
3. Breathing earth—the environment
4. Cool Science for Curious Kids
5. Geo Games
6. Lifeboat to Mars
7. Life Cycles
8. Life cycle—potatoes
9. Moon—Garfield teaches Lunar Cycle
10. NASA Kids Club
11. NASA City
12. Nature—explore it
13. Ocean Tracks
14. Ocean Currents—video from NASA

15. Plants—life cycle
16. Redwood Forests video
17. Science games I
18. Science Games II
19. Science Games—Bitesize
20. Science Games—BrainPop
21. Science info websites
22. Science—interactive activities
23. Science interactive—plates, etc
24. Simulations—varied
25. Solar System Video
26. Solar System in 3D
27. Space—write your name in galaxies
28. Stardate Online

29. Virtual tour (with pictures) of a zoo
30. Virtual tours
31. Virtual tour—undersea
32. Virtual weather, machines and surgery
33. Water Cycle Game

Spanish

Spanish resources
Stories in Spanish
Spanish words and phrases game

Stories

- Aesop's Fables
- Aesop Fables—no ads
- Audio stories
- Childhood Stories
- Classic Fairy Tales
- Edutainment games and stories
- Fairy Tales and Fables
- Fables—Aesop—nicely done
- Fables—beautiful
- Interactive storybook collection
- Listen/read—Free non-fic audio books
- Make Your Story
- Make Believe Comix
- Make your own Story II
- Make your story a newspaper clipping
- Make another story
- Mighty Book
- PBS Stories—Between the Lions
- Starfall
- Stories—CircleTime—international
- Stories read by actors
- Stories—non-text
- Story time—visual
- Stories—MeeGenius—read/to me
- Stories to read from PBS kids
- Stories to read—International Library
- Stories—Signed
- Stories to read for youngsters
- Storybook Maker
- Storytime for me
- Web-based Madlibs
- Ziggity Zoom Stories
- Zooburst—pop up stories

Technology

1. Animated GIF Creator
2. Computer basics
3. Computer Basics II
4. Computer Insides
5. Computer puzzle
6. Find the Technology
7. Graphic organizers
8. Kodu—game programming
9. NASA Kids Club
10. Newspaper—create a newspaper
11. Newspaper—create a newspaper clipping
12. Organize technology (drag and drop)
13. Parts of the computer
14. Posters, Newspapers, Comics—learn to create
15. Sketch Up Intro
16. Tab key—video on using
17. Videos on Computer Basics K-6

Virtual Tours

1. 360 Panorama of the world
2. Google World of Wonders
3. Virtual tour—White House on GE
4. Virtual tour of America—via Biplane

Word Study

1. Dolch Site Word Activities
2. Flash cards
3. Fact Fragment Frenzy—finding facts
4. Flash cards and more
5. Flash cards—mini and large
6. Grammar—Adjectives
7. Grammar games
8. Hangman
9. High-frequency words—hangman
10. High-frequency words—practice
11. High-frequency word games—k-2
12. Speechable
13. Spell by spinning the letters
14. Stories with Dolch Words
15. Visuwords
16. Vocabulary Fun
17. Vocabulary-Spelling City
18. Word and logic problems
19. Word clouds—ABCya
20. Word games—k-2
21. Word Study Games—Merriam Webster

Writing

1. Comic creator—Lego.com
2. Comic creator—ReadWriteThink
3. Comic creator—Arthur
4. Comic creator—Garfield
5. Comic Creator—Disney
6. Comic Creator—Boy's Life
7. Create a story
8. Comics, newspapers, posters—learn to create
9. Letter Generator
10. Garfield teaches Writing Skills
11. Make Believe Comix
12. Make your own Story
13. Make another story
14. Newspapers, posters, comics—learn to create
15. Writing games

For Teachers

1. Animations, assessments, charts, more
2. Art on your Whiteboard
3. Audio books—free—Project Gutenberg
4. Audio books—Ms. Noor—free—kid-oriented
5. 10 Technology Enhanced Book Reports
6. Brainstorming—Spicy Nodes
7. Children's University
8. Class badges
9. Classroom floorplan—for architect unit
10. Collection of websites
11. Cool Tools for School
12. Create a magazine cover
13. Create free activities and diagrams in a Flash!
14. Easy-to-navigate collection
15. Easy Techie Stuff for the Classroom
16. Enchanted Learning
17. Environmental footprint
18. FBI Kid-safe games
19. Google Earth Lesson Plans I
20. Google Earth Lesson Plans II
21. Google Earth in Math Curriculum
22. Graphic organizers
23. Graphic organizers II
24. Graphic Organizers III
25. Graphic organizers—all topics
26. Graphic organizers—Enchanted Learning
27. Graphic Organizers—for reading
28. Hollywood Sq/Jeopardy Templates
29. How to Videos for Web 2.0
30. Internet Movie Database
31. Jeopardy Labs
32. K-8 school-related videos. Tons of them
33. Miscellaneous links
34. Online quizzes you create, online grades
35. Parent Education Videos
36. Password creator
37. PBS Learning Resources
38. Poster maker—like an eye chart
39. Poster maker—like a road sign
40. Posters—8x10 at a time—simple
41. PowerPoint games for kids
42. PowerPoint Templates
43. Print Large Posters in 8x10 bits
44. Print Posters One Page at a Time

45. Publish the magazines
46. QR Codes
47. Random Team Generator
48. Rubrics I
49. Rubrics II
50. Rubrics III
51. Rubrics/Assessments—Kathy Schrock
52. Rubrics—for CCSS
53. Screen Capture—full webpage
54. Screencast-o-matic
55. So many Free online tools (Web 2.0)
56. Takk—create online fliers
57. Teacher Training Videos
58. Teach vocab—prefixes/suffixes
59. Technology use survey—interactive
60. Tests—create fill-in-the-blanks
61. Tools for studying writing
62. Training videos
63. Turn pictures into Videos—Easily
64. White Board—no sign in, no reg

Congratulations!

Has completed all requirements for 2nd grade Technology, including:

- Introductory Ms Word
- Introductory PowerPoint
- Introductory Publisher

- Introductory Web tools
- 2nd Grade graphic arts
- 2nd Grade Excel

- 2nd Grade Digital Citizenship
- 2nd Grade Google Earth
- 2nd Grade keyboarding

Signature

Date